I0160094

Book One

Understanding
Spoken
English

a focus on everyday language in context

Susan Boyer

Revised cover edition, 2014

Boyer Educational Resources 2003
reprinted 2005, 2007, 2008, 2009, 2013

Published by
Boyer Educational Resources

Phone/fax: + 61 (0)2 4739 1538
E-mail: boyer@eftel.net.au
Web address: www.boyereducation.com.au
            www.englishebooks.com

Acknowledgments

I would like to express my thanks to the following people for their contribution to the final presentation
of this book:

Firstly, I would like to thank all the teachers who trialed material contained in the original edition of this
book and suggested improvements. I wish to say thank you to Terry Stroble for his time and constructive
comments regarding North American usage of expressions included in this book.

I would like to thank Matthew Larwood for his creative illustrations. I would like to say thank
you to Darrell Hilton Productions for the production of the accompanying audio recordings and to
Jeanette Christian for proofreading. And of course, I am particularly indebted to the many students who
have given me the necessary insight into the language needs of English language learners around the
world.

Also, I want to thank my dear husband, Len, for his encouragement and support throughout the project, as
well as the many hours spent in the production of this resource.

Illustrations on pages 8 (pictures 1, 5, 7, 8, 9), 20, 30, 41, 42, 54, 75, 76, 86, 96 & 109 are by Matthew J Larwood.

The images used herein were obtained from IMSI's MasterClips Collection,
1895 Francisco Blvd. East, San Rafael, CA 94901-5506, USA.
(Except the kookaburra clipart which was obtained from Australian Graphics Selection, New Horizons,
Armidale. Australia.)

Boyer, Susan
Understanding Spoken English: a focus on everyday language in context
ISBN 1 877074 08 X

1. English language - Spoken English - Textbooks for foreign speakers.
2. English language - Spoken English - Problems, exercises, etc. I. Boyer Educational Resources
II Title

428.34

Boyer Educational Resources
PO Box 255, Glenbrook, 2773 Australia,
Phone/fax: + 61 (0)2 4739 1538

Dear English Language Student,

Welcome to *Understanding Spoken English – a focus on everyday language in context*. This book, along with its accompanying audio recording, has been designed to help you to understand English as it is spoken in 'everyday' situations in English speaking environments around the world. As a student of English as a second or foreign language, you are no doubt aware of the difference between the formally presented language of many textbooks and the speech you hear, outside the language classroom, in the English speaking media or in conversations with native English speakers.

As well as introducing and explaining the meaning of many widely used everyday expressions, each unit focuses on other aspects of English, such as the use of **contractions** (eg. *won't* rather than *will not*), **ellipsis** (incomplete sentences) and **intonation** (the rise and fall of the voice pitch). These features are distinctive characteristics of spoken (rather than written) English. You will also learn social conventions involved in everyday situations such as making a telephone call, dealing with service people and informal social interactions.

I sincerely hope you enjoy and benefit from using *Understanding Spoken English - a focus on everyday language in context*.

Susan Boyer

A note on English accents used in the audio recording

The conversations on the accompanying audio recording present speakers with a variety of different English accents as they are encountered in English speaking environments around the world. This is because it is very beneficial for students to become accustomed to the different accents of English speakers that will be encountered in the media, in international business contexts and social situations.

The intention of presenting different accents, however, is not to provide particular models for imitation but to *increase familiarity* with a variety of different accents.

It should be noted that, though the *accents* of the speakers vary, the vocabulary and grammar points presented in each unit of this book are those common to all varieties of 'native speaker' English.

ABOUT THIS BOOK

Understanding Spoken English has been designed so that you can work through it alone, without the help of a teacher, or in a classroom situation with other students. The book contains nine units of work, each based on a conversation about a particular topic. The units are divided into *six parts* that have been designed to introduce unfamiliar language, *step by step,* in a gradual and systematic way. The layout of the book is as follows:

Part 1 - Focus on listening for general understanding

Part 1 introduces the topic and invites you to listen to an everyday conversation and answer a few general questions by putting a tick next to the correct answers. You will be listening for *general* understanding of the conversation only. (You will not need to understand every word.) This is an important step as it will help you to realise that it's not always necessary to hear every word to understand the general meaning of a conversation. In some units, you are asked to check words in a dictionary, so have a dictionary nearby when you are studying.

Part 2 - Focus on reading & finding the meaning

In this section, you will *read* Conversation 1 as you listen again. When you have finished listening, your task is to *compare Conversation 1 with Conversation 2* (which will be next to Conversation 1). Conversation 1 contains the everyday expressions and Conversation 2 contains an interpretation of the expressions in Conversation 1. This section will help you to learn the *meaning* of the everyday expressions.

Part 3 - Focus on listening for detail

Now you will listen to Conversation 1 again and write in the missing words in the spaces as you hear them. Don't worry about spelling as this exercise focuses on your *listening skills* - you can check your spelling later. Listen to the conversation as many times as you like, then check your answers (and spelling) by comparing what you have written with Conversation 1.

Part 4 - Focus on listening and writing for reinforcement

This section reinforces (strengthens) your memory as you listen once more to Conversation 1 and tick the newly learnt everyday expressions on the list as you hear them. Then you are asked to look at the list of expressions (all taken from Conversation 1) and try to remember their meaning. Write in the ones that you can remember, then check your answers by reading Conversation 1 again or checking the reference list at the back of the book. This may seem like hard work but *writing* the meanings of the newly learnt expressions is a useful way of reinforcing what you have just heard and read.

Part 5 - Focus on language revision - crosswords

Now it's time to test yourself and see what you have learnt by trying the language revision and crossword activity. In this section, you are asked to use the newly learned expressions in a different context. In each unit you are asked to complete sentences with the appropriate expression and complete the crossword. The answers to the exercises can be found in the answer section of this book.

Part 6 - Focus on other aspects of spoken English

In this section, there will be exercises for you to complete and/or cultural advice for you to remember. This section focuses on aspects of spoken English (grammar, pronunciation etc.) that may make it difficult for learners to understand. Each unit focuses on conversation strategies or social conventions used by the speakers in Conversation 1 of that particular unit.

Language Reviews

After Unit 3, Unit 6 and Unit 9 you will find a language review that consists of pictures and sentences containing the 'everyday' expressions, which were introduced in the preceding units, for you to match together. This will help you to see how much you have remembered.

IMPORTANT NOTE TO STUDENTS

Please be aware that the meaning of colloquial language is *very dependent on the context or situation in which it is used.* 'Understanding Spoken English' has been designed to *introduce and explain* the meaning of colloquial expressions used by English speakers in the everyday situations presented in this book. However, because colloquial expressions can have different meanings in different situations, it is not recommended that students of English immediately begin using the newly introduced expressions indiscriminately. It would be much better to spend time becoming familiar with, and understanding the correct meaning of expressions in different situations *before you use them* in your conversations.

In this regard, the author and publisher of this book will not be responsible to any person, with regard to the misuse of language, caused directly or indirectly by the information presented in this book.

UNDERSTANDING SPOKEN ENGLISH – BOOK ONE

CONTENTS

CONTENTS

GLOSSARY OF LANGUAGE TERMS

Use this list as a reference while you are using this book.

adjective: a word which describes things (*black* car), people (*beautiful* girl), places (*multicultural* city) or events (*exciting* race), etc.

alphabet: The English alphabet consists of twenty six letters:
a, b, c, d, e, f, g, h, i, j, k, l, m, n, o, p, q, r, s, t, u, v, w, x, y, z.

These letters are categorised into **vowels**: a, e, i, o, u.
and **consonants**: b, c, d, f, g, h, j, k, l, m, n, p, q, r, s, t, v, w, x, y, z.
(The consonant letter 'y' can be pronounced as a vowel sound; for example: 'gym'.)

article: The words *'a', 'an', 'the'* are called articles.

auxiliary verb: a 'helper' verb which is used with another verb to form tense. (eg. *will* come, *did* come, *have* come) Modal auxiliary verbs are used with another verb to show mood or manner. (eg. *should* come, *might* come, *must* come).

discourse marker: Discourse markers **show connection** between what has already been said and what will come next in a stretch of discourse.. (eg.'...however,..', '*and I'm sure you'll agree...*'). A discourse marker is also a word or expression which shows the speaker's attitude to what is being said. eg. '*In fact,.....*', '*...and of course...*'

ellipsis: the omission of words from a sentence when the meaning is clear without them, due to the context of the conversation. eg. *Anything else? (meaning 'Is there any thing else? '*

imperative: base (simple) form of a verb, used at the beginning of a sentence, to give orders, instructions, directions. (eg. *Be* quiet; *Turn* left at the next corner).

intonation: Intonation refers to the way our voice goes up and down in pitch when speaking.

noun: a word which names **things**, (eg. car, sky); **places** (eg. New Zealand, ocean) **people** (eg. John, President), as well as **abstract things**, things we can't see but can experience/talk about. (eg. history, pain, ideas, education).

phrasal verb: A verb that consists of two parts: a base verb and an adverbial particle. eg. 'pick up', 'try on'

phonemic symbols: See the explanation below for 'sound symbols'.

pronoun: a word which is used in place of a noun. eg. *it, she, they*. (See Unit 3 - Part 6A, 6B)

schwa: The symbol 'ə', and the sound it represents, are referred to as 'schwa'. The symbol 'ə' (schwa) is used in most dictionaries to represent weak, unstressed syllables in words.

sound symbols: also called **phonemic symbols** – these symbols represent the sounds of English. English sounds are generally divided into two main categories: **vowel** sounds, and **consonant** sounds. The vowel sounds can be further divided into simple vowel sounds and **diphthong** sounds. Diphthongs can be defined as 'two vowel sounds linked or glided together within a syllable'. For example, the vowel sound in the word 'v<u>oi</u>ce' consists of two linked vowels sounds and is represented by the symbol /ɔɪ/.

See the Phonemic Chart of English Sounds on page 132 that shows the sound symbols of English, along with example words to demonstrate each sound.

GLOSSARY OF LANGUAGE TERMS

stress: In spoken language, **stress** refers to the emphasis of a word or syllable within a word.

word stress: In words with more than one syllable, one sound is usually stronger (spoken more clearly) than the other(s). The term, **stressed syllable**, refers to the strongest (primary) sound in words of more than one syllable.

sentence stress: Words which carry the main message of the sentence contain *stressed* syllables. Stressing the important words helps the listener to hear the message of the speaker. eg. I _want_ to go _home_.

syllable: Spoken words are formed with **syllables**, meaning **units of sound.** A syllable is a unit of unbroken sound, generally containing a vowel sound.

verb: a word which shows **action**.   eg. He *ran* all the way.
or **state/experience**.   eg. She *is* a student. I *feel* cold.

‘Base form’ can refer to the simple present form of the verb. eg. **be, go, see.**

verb tenses: Tenses show the **time** of an action, event or condition. Some examples are:

past simple tense: indicates finished past action. eg. He *went* to Asia last year.

present perfect tense: a) used for an action/experience which began in the past and has continued to the present. eg. I *have lived* here since 1998. eg. 1998

b) used when a past action/experience (which happened at an unspecified time) has present significance.

eg.. He *has been* to Asia.

present simple tense: a) indicates a present condition/fact.

eg. I *am* hungry.   eg.

b) indicates a present routine. eg. I *work* four days each week. eg.

present progressive: (also called present continuous) a verb form made with *am/are/is +...ing*.
a) This tense is used to talk about an action which is happening at the time of speaking. eg. We *are waiting* for him.
b) The present progressive is also used to refer to a future arrangement.
eg. He *is leaving* tomorrow.

future simple tense: will +verb indicates future time. eg. I think, it *will rain* tomorrow.

vowel sounds: See notes under 'sound symbols' on the previous page.

NOTE:
This list is not intended as a complete guide. Refer to a comprehensive grammar book for more details.

UNIT 1

STARTING SOMETHING NEW

We all learn new things throughout our lives - sometimes because we want to and sometimes because we have to. How do you feel about learning new things? Most people have 'mixed feelings' about starting new things. This means they often feel nervous and excited at the same time.

Listening for general understanding

Listen to this conversation between friends who are talking about starting something new. (Unit 1 on the audio recording.) The conversation contains everyday expressions that will be explained later in the unit - so don't worry if you don't understand every word. This time you are listening for a general understanding of the topic. As you listen, tick the correct answers below. (There may be more than one correct answer.) When you have finished you can check your answers on page 110.

1) Chris is telephoning Lee to ask about:

        a) a new job

        b) a new language course

        c) a new hobby

2) Lee suggests that Chris should do:

        a) an accountancy course

        b) a computer course

        c) a cooking course

3) Chris says:

        a) he is too old to learn new things

        b) he already knows how to do it

        c) he will enquire about a course this week

Now, we'll look at the everyday expressions used in the conversation – turn to the next page.

CONVERSATION 1 (with everyday expressions)

◂◂ Replay Conversation 1
Read this conversation as you listen to the audio recording. Do you know what the _underlined_ words mean? They are colloquial or 'everyday' expressions.

Lee: Hello.

Chris: Hello Lee. It's Chris here. I thought I'd **give you a buzz** and see how you're going in your new job.

Lee: Oh hi Chris. It's good to hear from you. I'm **getting into the swing of things** now thanks. I had a few **hassles** at first - you know everything was different. In the first week I thought the job **was beyond** me. I **couldn't make head nor tail of** the accounts system but I **stuck at it** and I'm going well now.

Chris: **Good for you**!

Lee: Thanks. What've you been **up to** anyway?

Chris: Not much. I'm **in a rut** in my job really. But I've been thinking about getting some training and going for a better job too.

Lee: Yes, you should. Why don't you do a computer course?

Chris: I don't really like the idea of studying again - it's so long since I left school. I **don't** really **know the first thing** about computer technology. I mean, what if everyone else in the class **catches on** quicker than me. I'm getting a bit old to learn new things.

Lee: Oh, **come off it!** **Tons** of people study as adults these days. Everyone in the class will be **in the same boat. Go on** Chris! Once you start, I'm sure you'll soon **get the hang of it**.

Chris: OK. You've **talked me into it**. I'll enquire about courses this week.

Lee: Good on you! Look, I'd better get back to work now - we're pretty busy today but I'll call you next week to see how you're **getting along**.

Chris: OK. I'll talk to you then. Thanks for the encouragement!

Lee: **See you**…and good luck.

Now let's see what the underlined expressions mean - look at the next page.

CONVERSATION 2 (explanation of everyday expressions)

Compare Conversation 1 with Conversation 2 - You will see that some of the words are different but the meaning is the same in both conversations. Find the underlined expressions in Conversation 1, then underline the words with the same meaning in Conversation 2. For example: *give you a buzz* (Conversation 1) = *call you on the telephone* (Conversation 2)

Lee: Hello.

Chris: Hello Lee. It's Chris here. I thought I'd call you on the telephone and see how you're going in your new job.

Lee: Oh hi Chris. It's good to hear from you. I'm becoming familiar with the usual way of doing things now thanks. I had a few problems/difficulties at first - you know everything was different. In the first week I thought the job was too difficult for me. I couldn't understand anything about the accounts system but I kept trying and I'm going well now.

Chris: Congratulations!

Lee: Thanks. What've you been doing anyway?

Chris: Not much. I'm in a boring pattern of doing things in my job really. But I've been thinking about getting some training and going for a better job too.

Lee: Yes, you should. Why don't you do a computer course?

Chris: I don't really like the idea of studying again - it's so long since I left school. I don't really know anything about computer technology. I mean, what if everyone else in the class learns/understands quicker than me. I'm getting a bit old to learn things.

Lee: Oh, I don't agree with you! A lot of people study as adults these days. Everyone in the class will be in the same situation. You should do it, Chris! Once you start, I'm sure you'll soon understand what to do.

Chris: OK. You've convinced me/shown me good reasons why I should do what you suggest. I'll enquire about courses this week.

Lee: Good on you! Look, I'd better get back to work now - we're pretty busy today but I'll call you next week to see how you're progressing/managing.

Chris: OK. I'll talk to you then. Thanks for the encouragement!

Lee: Goodbye......and good luck!

Important note:
The language used in Conversation 2 (above) may seem easier to understand when compared with Conversation 1. However, the 'everyday' expressions used in Conversation 1 are used extensively by speakers of English. Therefore it is beneficial to become familiar with the everyday expressions used by the speakers in **Conversation 1**.

◄◄ **Replay Conversation 1**

Listen to the conversation again and fill in the missing words. You may have to listen more than once. (Don't worry about your spelling as this exercise focuses on listening skills - you can check your spelling later.)

Lee: Hello.

Chris: Hello Lee. It's Chris here. I thought I'd **give you a** _____ and see how you're going in your new job.

Lee: Oh hi Chris. It's good to hear from you. I'm **getting into the** _____ **of things** now thanks. I had a few **hassles** at first - you know everything was different. In the first week I thought the job **was** _____ me. I **couldn't make** _____ **nor** _____ **of** the accounts system but I _____ **at it** and I'm going well now.

Chris: **Good for you**!

Lee: Thanks. What've you been _____ **to** anyway?

Chris: Not much. I'm **in a** _____ in my job really. But I've been thinking about getting some training and going for a better job too.

Lee: Yes, you should. Why don't you do a computer course?

Chris: I don't really like the idea of studying again - it's so long since I left school. I **don't** really **know the** _____ **thing** about computer technology. I mean, what if everyone else in the class **catches** _____ quicker than me. I'm getting a bit old to learn new things.

Lee: Oh, **come** _____ **it!** **Tons** of people study as adults these days. Everyone in the class will be **in the same** _____. **Go on** Chris! Once you start, I'm sure you'll soon **get the** _____ **of it**.

Chris: OK. You've **talked me** _____ **it**. I'll enquire about courses this week.

Lee: Good on you! Look, I'd better get back to work now - we're pretty busy today but I'll call you next week to see how you're **getting** _____.

Chris: OK. I'll talk to you then. Thanks for the encouragement!

Lee: _____ **you**…and good luck!

Now check your answers by comparing this page with CONVERSATION 1.

In order to become more familiar with these new everyday expressions:

◀◀ **Replay Conversation 1**
1) **Listen and tick the boxes** ☑ **next to the expressions as you hear them.**
2) **Write the definitions you can remember. (The first one has been done as an example.)**
   Check your answers with the reference list on page 122.

☐ give (you) a buzz.....................……   _call (you) on the telephone_

☐ getting into the swing of things……….

☐ hassles...................................

☐ beyond (someone)...........................

☐ *not* make head or tail of (something)…

☐ stuck at it..................................

☐ Good for you!...............................

☐ What've you been up to?...............…

☐ in a rut …………………………......

☐ *don't* know the first thing about (something)

☐ catch on..................................

☐ Come off it!.................................

☐ tons...

☐ in the same boat...............................

☐ Go on!.................................

☐ get the hang of it.............................

☐ talked (me) into it..........................

☐ getting along ……………………….

☐ See you.....................................

LANGUAGE NOTES

1. The word **'buzz'** (used as a noun) can have several meanings, depending on the context
   in which it is used. It can mean 'a low, continuous noise produced by an insect'.
   It can mean **'a call on the telephone'**, as in the example in the conversation of this unit.
   To **give/get a buzz** from doing something can mean to **give/get a thrill or good feeling**.
   eg. 'I get a buzz from helping people.'
   The expression '**Buzz off!**' is an impolite way of saying '**Go away!**'

2. The expressions **not** make head nor tail of (something), **not** know the first thing about (something)
   are usually expressed in the negative form.

3. The expression **getting along** meaning *progressing/managing*, can also be expressed as
   getting on. eg. 'How are you **getting along** in your job?' or 'How are you **getting on** in your job?'

CROSSWORD - LANGUAGE REVISION

Complete the sentences, choosing from the everyday expressions that are listed in the box below.
You can use the clues in brackets ( ) at the end of each sentence to help you.
Then complete the crossword using the everyday expressions you have written.
The first one has been done as an example.

head nor tail	stick at it	~~get the hang of~~	tons	catch on	getting along
in a rut	the first thing	swing	beyond me	buzz	same boat

ACROSS

1) You'll soon **_get the hang of_** this game. (understand what to do)
3) It's easier to _____ ___ to new things if you relax and enjoy learning. (learn/understand)
5) I'll give you a _____ tonight and we can make arrangements for tomorrow. (call on the telephone)
7) I can't make _____ ____ _____ of this grammar book. (understand anything)
9) There're always _____ of people at the beach in Summer. (a lot of)
11) I don't think he'll get a driving licence. He doesn't seem to know _____ _____ _____ about driving. (know anything)

DOWN

2) I'm ___ __ _____. I need to change my life and do something more interesting. (in a boring pattern of doing things)
4) This course is difficult but I'm going to _____ ___ ___. I'm sure it will get easier. (keep trying)
6) I practise English everyday and now I'm getting into the _____ of things. (becoming familiar with the usual way of doing things)
8) How are you _____ _____ in your new job? (progressing/managing)
10) This textbook is _____ ____. (too difficult for)
12) Everyone who has started their life again in a new country is in the _____ _____ . (same situation)

(Answers: page 110)

FOCUS ON SPOKEN LANGUAGE

A) Spoken words and syllables

- Spoken words are formed with syllables (or units of sound).

- A syllable is formed when individual sounds are pronounced together to form one unit of unbroken sound within a word. Each syllable generally contains a vowel sound.

- A word may contain one or more syllables.

    For example: *come* = one syllable; *welcome* = two syllables; *unwelcome* = three syllables

Read the first few words of Conversation 1 below. Which word has two syllables?

'Hello Lee. It's Chris here.'

(Answer: page 110)

B) Contracted words in spoken English

In conversational English, speakers use 'contractions'. This means they link two (or more) words together into one word. For example, instead of saying, *It is...* they say, *It's...*
Contracted words are often pronounced as one syllable but there are exceptions, as you will see in the exercise which follows.

◀◀ **Replay Conversation 1**
Listen to Conversation 1 again and circle the contractions used in the conversation (page 10) as you hear them. Notice the way the contractions are pronounced. Then do the following exercise.

Write the contracted form of these groups of words that have been used in Conversation 1. Notice the correct position for the apostrophe (') when you check your answers on page 110.

	Full form	Contraction	How many syllables in the contracted form?
For example:	I would	*I'd*	1
	you are		
	I am		
	could not		
	what have		
	do not		
	it is		
	you will		
	you have		
	I had		
	we are		
	I will		

Answers page: 110

- Note: Contractions are not generally used in formal writing.

C) Developing awareness of the stress patterns of English

As you have learnt, spoken words are formed with *syllables.* A word may contain only one syllable, as in the words, 'is', 'on', 'at'. However, words may have two or more syllables. For example: *for* = one syllable; *forgot* = two syllables; *forgotten* = three syllables.

In words of two or more syllables, one syllable is spoken more clearly or strongly than others. The most strongly pronounced syllable is called the *stressed* syllable. Look at the following two-syllable words as examples.

In the following words, the **first** syllable is **stressed.**

<u>bett</u>er
<u>sys</u>tem

In the following words, the **second** syllable is **stressed.**

a<u>long</u>
a<u>ccounts</u>

In Unit 2 you will practice using your dictionary to learn the stress patterns of new words.

D) Names and syllables

The speakers in Conversation 1 (page 10) are friends and therefore use given names, 'Chris' and 'Lee' when speaking to each other, rather than family names (also called surnames). The names 'Chris' and 'Lee' each have one syllable. However, 'Chris' is a shortened (abbreviated) form of 'Christopher', a male name, which has three syllables: Chris-to-pher.

What about you?

- When introducing yourself in an informal situation, do you use your given name or surname?

- When speaking with friends, do you use your given name or surname (family name)?

- How many syllables does your given name contain?

- How many syllables does your surname name contain?

- How many syllables does your friend's (or classmate's) given name contain?

Pronouncing names correctly - practice

It is important to remember the correct pronunciation of the names of people you meet. As you have learnt, it is necessary to know how many syllables a word contains in order to pronounce it correctly. It is also important to know which syllable is stressed.

- Write the names of people in your class
  (or people you work with) on a piece of paper.

- Ask them to pronounce their name slowly.

- Mark the syllables by drawing a line between each syllable
  and underline the most strongly stressed syllable. For example, show Christopher as <u>Chris</u>/to/pher.

- Check with them that you are pronouncing their names correctly.

NOTE ON TELEPHONE LANGUAGE

When we call people we know on the telephone, we often begin the conversation by saying '*Hello, this is Susan.*' or '*Hello, it's Susan here.*' We never say, '*I am Susan.*'
Notice how Chris introduced his call to Lee in Conversation 1 (page 10).

However, when making a business call, we would introduce ourselves using our surname.
For example: '*Hello, this is Susan Boyer...*' or if it's the initial call, '*Hello, my name is Susan Boyer...*'

E) Stress in sentences

In this section, you will see how *stress* is used in spoken English sentences. You will see how some words are spoken more *clearly* and *loudly* than the other words in a sentence. These words are called *stressed* words. The stressed words convey the main message of the speaker. To put more simply, speakers *stress* the words they want their listeners to focus on.

On the other hand, words that do *not* carry the main message of the speaker are spoken quickly and softly. They are *un*stressed or reduced. For this reason, spoken English can be compared to music where some sounds are **l o n g** and **loud**; some sounds are short and soft.

◀◀ Replay Conversation 1

Listen and read the first two sentences from the beginning of Conversation 1 and notice the stress pattern. The *stressed* words are marked by the symbol •.

•   •   •   •   •   •   •   •   •   •   •

He**llo Lee**. It's **Chris here**. I **thought** I'd **give** you a **buzz** and **see** how you're **going** in your **new job**.

Did you hear that the stressed words marked • were spoken more loudly and clearly than the other words?

(Note: In stressed words with two syllables (or more), one syllable has the main stress. For example, in the word 'going', the first syllable is stressed, but the second syllable is unstressed.)

Did you notice that the words that do *not* carry the main message of the speaker are spoken quickly and softly? They are unstressed. These words, they are referred to as *weak* or *reduced*.

Note:

It is not absolutely necessary for learners of English to use these features of spoken English to *be understood by others*. However, the use of correct stress patterns is important in developing the natural flow of English speech. It is also very important for students to be aware of these stress features of spoken language in order for them *to understand* the natural speech of native English speakers in the media and in business and social situations.

Reference page
Understanding the Stress Patterns of English

Word Stress

- Spoken words contain *syllables*. A syllable is formed by the linking of individual sounds within a word to form one unit of unbroken sound. A word can contain one or more syllables. For example: *come* = one syllable; *welcome* = two syllables; *welcoming* = three syllables.

- In spoken English, some syllables in words are spoken more clearly or strongly than others. Strong or prominent sounds are called *stressed* syllables. For example, in the word **wel**come which has two syllables, the first syllable is stressed.

  The weaker or reduced syllables are called *unstressed* syllables and are often represented in dictionaries by the symbol /ə/. This sound and its symbol /ə/ is called the *schwa*. For example, the pronunciation of the word 'welcome' will be shown in the dictionary as /ˈwelkəm/

  Note: Other symbols, such as /ɪ/, may also be used to represent an unstressed vowel sound. For example, the word 'hectic', will be shown in the dictionary as /ˈhektɪk/

  Unit 2 will provide practice with using your dictionary to learn the stress patterns of new words.

Stress within sentences

- In spoken English sentences, words that give **important information** contain *stressed* syllables. These are generally **content words**, such as nouns (things), verbs (actions) and adjectives (describers).

  Words which *don't* carry the main message of the speaker (ie. structure words like *the, of, a*) are generally *unstressed*. These unstressed words are spoken softly and quickly.

  Look at the following sentence as an example:

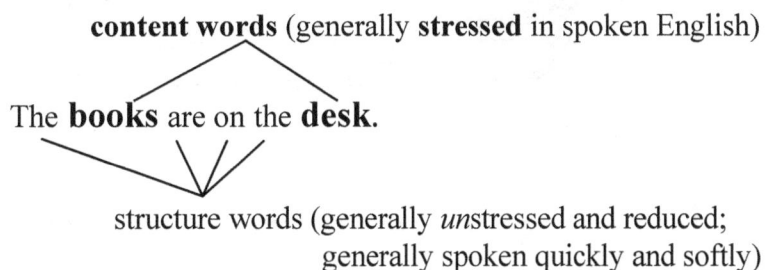

  content words (generally **stressed** in spoken English)

  The **books** are on the **desk**.

  structure words (generally *un*stressed and reduced; generally spoken quickly and softly)

  In Unit 4 you will learn more about strong and weak syllables in spoken English.

You can learn more about the stress patterns of English in the book,
'Understanding English Pronunciation - an integrated practice course'.
See details on the final page of this book.

UNIT 2

TALKING ABOUT THE FAMILY

Listening for general understanding

This conversation contains colloquial or everyday expressions relating to family life. These will be explained later in the unit so don't worry if you don't understand every word of the conversation. This time you are only listening for general understanding of the topic. Listen to the conversation between friends (Unit 2 on the audio recording) and decide which of the photographs on the opposite page the speakers are talking about. (Answers: page 110)

Before you listen to the conversation again, check these words in a dictionary if you are not familiar with their meaning. (Answers: page 110)

in-laws	characteristic	relationship	(cultural) background	tolerant

◀◀ Replay Conversation 1

Listen to the conversation again and tick the correct answer below. You may need to listen more than once. When you have finished, you can check your answers on page 110.

1) The photograph that the speakers are looking at
was taken:

      a) last week

      b) a few months ago

      c) a few years ago

2) What is David's health problem?

      a) an eye problem

      b) a hearing problem

      c) a heart problem

3) What has caused the problem between Jean's
daughters-in-law ?

      a) business problems

      b) cultural differences

      c) health problems

Now, we'll look at the everyday expressions used in the conversation – turn to the next page.

CONVERSATION 1 (with everyday expressions)

◀◀ **Replay Conversation 1**
Read this conversation as you listen to the audio recording. Do you know what the _underlined_ **words mean? They are colloquial or 'everyday' expressions.**

Merv: Are these your sons, Jean? I haven't seen them **for ages**.

Jean: Yes, that photo was taken a few months ago.

Merv: John hasn't changed a bit. He's **the image of** his father, isn't he?

Jean: Yes, he is. He **takes after** his father, that's for sure.

Merv: What's he doing **these days**?

Jean: He's **followed in his father's footsteps** too and works in the family importing business. He's living overseas at the moment.

Merv: Oh really? How does he like it?

Jean: It was difficult for him at first because he had to **start from scratch**, you know, finding somewhere to live and making new friends. He's **settled in** now though and he loves it.

Merv: That's good to hear. And how's David?

Jean: Well I'm sorry to say he hasn't been very well. He's been having problems with his heart. We're very worried about him because heart disease **runs in** our family you know.

Merv: Really? I didn't know that.

Jean: Yes, my younger brother **passed away** last year after a heart attack.

Merv: Oh, I'm very sorry to hear that, Jean. He wasn't very old, was he?

Jean: No, he wasn't - only thirty-eight. At least David knows about the problem and he can look after himself.

Merv: Mm. And do the boys **keep in touch**? I remember they used to be very close.

Jean: Yes they do - but not as much as before they were married. Their wives don't **get along**, so it's a bit of a **sticky** situation, you know.

Merv: That's not good! In-laws can be a problem sometimes…

Jean: Yes, they can sometimes. This problem's because they're from different cultural backgrounds.

Merv: **You're kidding**?

Jean: Mm. It's **a tough one** because we **brought up** the boys to be tolerant about other cultures and to **get on with** everyone.

Merv: Well let's hope their ideas **rub off on** their wives.

Jean: Yes, let's hope so.

Now let's see what the underlined expressions mean - look at the next page.

CONVERSATION 2 (explanation of everyday expressions)

Compare Conversation 1 with Conversation 2 - **You will see that some of the words are different but the meaning is the same in both conversations. Find the underlined expressions in Conversation 1, then underline the words with the same meaning in Conversation 2. For example:** <u>for ages</u> **(Conversation 1)** = <u>for a long time</u> **(Conversation 2)**

Merv: Are these your sons Jean? I haven't seen them <u>for a long time</u>.

Jean: Yes, that photo was taken a few months ago.

Merv: John hasn't changed a bit. He's the same in appearance as his father, isn't he?

Jean: Yes, he is. He is similar to his father, that's for sure.

Merv: What's he doing at the present time?

Jean: He's done the same as his father did too and works in the family importing business. He's living overseas at the moment.

Merv: Oh really? How does he like it?

Jean: It was difficult for him at first because he had to start from the beginning without help, you know, finding somewhere to live and making new friends. He's become established now though and he loves it.

Merv: That's good to hear. And how's David?

Jean: Well, I'm sorry to say he hasn't been very well. He's been having problems with his heart. We're very worried about him because heart disease is a common characteristic in our family, you know.

Merv: Really? I didn't know that.

Jean: Yes, my younger brother died last year after a heart attack.

Merv: Oh, I'm very sorry to hear that, Jean. He wasn't very old, was he?

Jean: No, he wasn't - only thirty-eight. At least David knows about the problem and he can look after himself.

Merv: Mm. And do the boys communicate regularly? I remember they used to be very close.

Jean: Yes they do - but not as much as before they were married. Their wives don't like each other, so it's a bit of a difficult situation, you know.

Merv: That's not good! In-laws can be a problem sometimes…

Jean: Yes, they can sometimes. This problem's because they are from different cultural backgrounds.

Merv: Really? That is surprising.

Jean: Mm. It's a difficult problem because we trained and educated the boys to be tolerant about other cultures and to be friendly with everyone.

Merv: Well let's hope their ideas are transferred to/have influence on their wives.

Jean: Yes, let's hope so.

Important note:
The language used in Conversation 2 (above) may seem easier to understand when compared with Conversation 1. However, the 'everyday' expressions used in Conversation 1 are used extensively by speakers of English. Therefore it is beneficial to become familiar with the everyday expressions used by the speakers in **Conversation 1**.

◄◄ **Replay Conversation 1**
Listen to the conversation again and fill in the missing words. You may have to listen more than once. Don't worry about your spelling as this exercise focuses on listening skills.

Merv: Are these your sons Jean? I haven't seen them **for** _____ .

Jean: Yes, that photo was taken a few months ago.

Merv: John hasn't changed a bit. He's **the** _____ **of** his father, isn't he?

Jean: Yes, he is. He **takes** _____ his father, that's for sure.

Merv: What's he doing **these days?**

Jean: He's _____ **in his father's footsteps** too and works in the family importing business. He's living overseas at the moment.

Merv: Oh really? How does he like it?

Jean: It was difficult for him at first because he had to **start from** _____ , you know, finding somewhere to live and making new friends. He's **settled in** now though and he loves it.

Merv: That's good to hear. And how's David?

Jean: Well I'm sorry to say he hasn't been very well. He's been having problems with his heart. We're very worried about him because heart disease _____ **in** our family you know.

Merv: Really? I didn't know that.

Jean: Yes, my younger brother _____ **away** last year after a heart attack.

Merv: Oh, I'm very sorry to hear that, Jean. He wasn't very old, was he?

Jean: No, he wasn't - only thirty-eight. At least David knows about the problem and he can look after himself.

Merv: Mm. And do the boys **keep in** _____ ? I remember they used to be very close.

Jean: Yes they do - but not as much as before they were married.
Their wives don't _____ **along**, so it's a bit of a _____ situation, you know.

Merv: That's not good! In-laws can be a problem sometimes…

Jean: Yes, they can sometimes. This problem's because they're from different cultural backgrounds.

Merv: **You're kidding?**

Jean: Mm. It's **a tough** _____ because we **brought** _____ the boys to be tolerant about other cultures and to _____ **on with** everyone.

Merv: Well let's hope their ideas **rub** _____ **on** their wives.

Jean: Yes, let's hope so.

Now check your answers by comparing this page with
CONVERSATION 1.

◄◄Replay Conversation 1

In order to become more familiar with these new everyday expressions:

1) Listen and tick the boxes ☑ next to the expressions as you hear them.

2) Write in the definitions you can remember. (One has been done as an example.)

   Check your answers with the reference list on page 123.

☐ for ages... *for a long time*

☐ the image of (someone)...................

☐ take after...

☐ these days...

☐ follow in (someone's) footsteps......

☐ start from scratch.........................…

☐ settled in..

☐ runs in (the family).........................

☐ passed away......................................

☐ keep in touch...................................

☐ don't get along.................................

☐ sticky (situation)..............................

☐ You're kidding.................................

☐ a tough one......................................

☐ brought up (children)...................

☐ get on with.......................................

☐ rub off on...

LANGUAGE NOTE:

The expression, '**not** get <u>along</u> with (someone)' can also be expressed as '**not** get <u>on</u> with (someone)'.

PRONUNCIATION NOTE:

Many English words, containing the letter 'a' may be pronounced as a short sound /æ/ or a long sound /ɑ:/ depending on which variety of English is being spoken. Two examples, taken from Conversation 1, are the words '*passed*' and '*last*'. (See more examples on page 131.)

Spelling	Examples of pronunciation differences of the letter 'a' in the following words.	
passed last	/pæst/ ⎫ /læst/ ⎭ Some speakers of English pronounce these words with the short vowel sound /æ/ as in bl<u>a</u>ck h<u>a</u>t 🎩	/pɑ:st/ ⎫ /lɑ:st/ ⎭ Some speakers of English pronounce these words with the long vowel sound /ɑ:/ as in l<u>a</u>rge h<u>ea</u>rt ♥

The variation in pronunciation, shown in the examples above, is generally well known and therefore, does not cause communication problems between speakers of different varieties of English.

CROSSWORD - LANGUAGE REVISION

Complete the sentences, choosing from the everyday expressions listed below. You can use the clues in brackets ( ) at the end of each sentence to help you. Then complete the crossword using the everyday expressions you have written. The first one has been done as an example.

brought up	get along	sticky	runs in	~~passed away~~	ages	image
rub off on	take after	settle in	keep in touch		start from scratch	

ACROSS

1) My grandfather ***passed away*** before I was born. (died)
3) I was _____ ___ by my parents to believe that honesty and hard work are very important. (trained and educated in the family)
5) Your daughter is the _____ of you. (same in appearance)
7) When we moved here, it took us a year to _____ ___ and make new friends. (become established)
9) Poor eyesight _____ ___ our family so most of us have to wear glasses. (is a common characteristic)
11) When we moved overseas, we had to _____ _____ _____ because we didn't know anyone. (start from the beginning without help)

DOWN

2) My brother and sister-in-law don't ____ _____ . (***don't*** like each other)
4) I hope your good habits _____ ____ ____ your brother. (influence/transfer to)
6) I haven't had a holiday for _____.(a long time)
8) I _____ _____ my mother but my sister takes after my father. (am similar to)
10) Do you still _____ ____ _____ with your friends from school? (communicate regularly)
12) My parents don't get along with my fiance, so our wedding could be a bit _____.(difficult)

(Answers: page 111)

FOCUS ON SPOKEN LANGUAGE

A) 'Question tags' in conversational speech

In spoken English, we sometimes use *'question tags'* at the end of a sentence to make it more conversational. For example, 'It's very hot today, *isn't it?*' (The last part, *'isn't it?'* is called the question tag).

- Look at Conversation 1 of this unit again (page 22).
- Find Merv's statements with a question tag at the end.
- Write them in the space below. You should be able to find two sentences with question tags.
- Look at the short replies that Jean gives and write them next to Merv's sentences.
  Jean's first reply has been written for you. (Answers: page 111)

Merv's Statements (with question tag)	Jean's reply
1) _____	Yes, he is.
2) _____	_____

NOTICE THE PATTERN

Statement	Question tag	Short reply
He *is* the image of his father,	*isn't* he?	Yes, he *is.*

If the first part of the sentence has a *positive* verb, the question tag is *negative*.
If the first part of the sentence has a *negative* verb, the question tag is *positive.*
When the speaker is using a question tag to be conversational, the reply agrees with the first part of the sentence. For example:

He *wasn't* very old,	*was* he?	No, he *wasn't.*

Practise adding a tag to these statements. (Firstly, notice the verb in the first part of the sentence - is it positive or negative?) Then add a short reply, agreeing with the statement.

a) Inlaws can be a problem sometimes, _____? _____

b) It was cold today, ..._____? _____

c) This classroom isn't very big,.........._____? _____

(Answers: page 111)

SUMMARY - USING QUESTION TAGS

Generally, when we use question tags to be friendly or conversational, we are <u>not</u> asking for information - we expect our listener to agree with us.

For example:	Reply
'Winter will be here soon, won't it?'	'Yes, it certainly will.'
'It isn't very busy today, is it?'	'No, it isn't.'

There will be revision on 'question tags' in a later unit of this book.

B) Hearing and pronouncing syllables correctly

In Unit 1 you learnt that:

- Spoken words are formed with syllables (or units of sound).
- A syllable is formed when individual sounds are pronounced together to form one unit of unbroken sound within a word.
- A word may contain one or more syllables.
  For example: *come* = one syllable; *welcome* = two syllables; *unwelcome* = three syllables

It's important to be able to *hear* how many syllables a word contains in order to be able to *pronounce* it correctly.

LISTENING PRACTICE

◄◄ Replay Conversation 1

- Listen to the first part of Conversation 1 (printed below) again. As you listen, decide how many syllables the underlined words contain.

- Write the number of syllables above the words. The first one has been done as an example. Pause the recording while you write your answer. You can check your answers on page 111.

Merv: Are **these** your **sons**, Jean? I haven't seen them for **ages**.

Jean: Yes, that **photo** was **taken** a few months **ago**.

Merv: John hasn't changed a bit. He's the **image** of his **father**, isn't he?

Jean: Yes, he is. He **takes** after his father, that's for **sure**.

Merv: What's he **doing** these days?

Jane: He's **followed** in his father's footsteps too and works in the **family importing business**. He's living **overseas** at the **moment**.

Note: The words '**family**' and '**business**' can be pronounced as two or three syllables. However, when spoken quickly as in Conversation 1, they are pronounced as two syllables. eg. **fam**(i)**ly**; **bus**(i)**ness**

* For information on the pronunciation of words with 'ed' endings see Unit 8, Part 6.

C) Hearing and using correct stress in words

In words with more than one syllable, one syllable is usually stronger (spoken more clearly) than the other syllables. Using the correct stress in words is essential to correct pronunciation.

Stress in words refers to the strongest (primary) sound in words of more than one syllable.

Important Note

A good dictionary will provide very useful information on how to pronounce words correctly. At the beginning (or end) of your dictionary, near the Pronunciation Key, you will see an explanation of how *stress* is shown on all words listed in the dictionary.

Dictionaries use various symbols to show which syllable should be stressed, so it's important to check which symbol *your* dictionary uses. For example, in the word *seven* (which contains two syllables), the stress is on the first syllable. Look at the way this may be shown in a dictionary.

*some dictionaries show a small stress mark ' *before and above* the stressed syllable. eg. 'seven.
*some dictionaries show a small stress mark ' *after and above* the stressed syllable.   eg. sev'en.
*some dictionaries use *a line under* the stressed syllable, to show the stressed part.   eg. seven

To avoid confusion, check which way *your* dictionary shows word stress.

How does *your* dictionary show that the first syllable is stressed in the word *seven*? _____

DICTIONARY PRACTICE

Using your dictionary, check the following two-syllable words and show the stressed syllable, using the stress symbol from your dictionary. Then check if you can hear the stress, by listening to the words in the first section of Conversation 1 again.

ages   *taken*   *ago*   *image*   *family*   *business*   *moment*

DICTIONARY CHECKLIST

- Does your dictionary give clear, simple definitions of words or expressions, with examples of how the word may be used in different contexts?
- Does your dictionary have a pronunciation key that gives clear examples of pronunciation?
- Does your dictionary have a simple way of showing word stress?

Pronunciation Note

There are some words in which the word stress differs between British and North American English, so always refer to your dictionary if in doubt.

UNIT 3

TALKING ABOUT OTHER PEOPLE

In English there is a saying, 'It takes all kinds to make a world' (sometimes we say, 'It takes all kinds...') This means that every person is different and we have to accept these differences. However, sometimes that's not so easy when we have problems with other people; especially people we have to see often!

Listening for general understanding

Listen to the conversation (Unit 3 on the audio recording) between two friends who live in the same area. They are talking about other people who live nearby. The conversation contains everyday expressions that will be explained later in the unit - so don't worry if you don't understand every word. This time you are only listening for a general understanding of the topic. As you listen, tick the correct answers below. You can check your answers on page 112.

1) At the beginning of the conversation, Jane is:

      a) very happy.

      b) not very happy.

2) During the conversation, Jane says she:

      a) doesn't like any of the people in her street.

      b) likes the people living on both sides of her house.

      c) likes the people who live on one side of her house but doesn't like the people on the other side.

3) During the conversation, Bob says:

      a) he hasn't met the new people yet.

      b) he has met the new people.

4) Jane says that the person who lives in number 5:

      a) likes gardening.

      b) is probably watching TV.

      c) is probably watching her and Bob.

Now, we'll look at the everyday expressions used in the conversation – turn to the next page.

CONVERSATION 1 (with everyday expressions)

◀◀ **Replay Conversation 1**
Read this conversation as you listen to the audio recording. Do you know what the
underlined **words mean? They are colloquial or 'everyday' expressions.**

Bob: Hi Jane. How are you?

Jane: I'm feeling a bit **out of sorts** this morning, Bob. I **didn't sleep a wink** last night. The people next door were making **a racket** again until **all hours**. They **couldn't care less** about anyone else. I'm **fed up** with the situation but I don't know what to do about it.

Bob: Why don't you **give them a piece of your mind**?

Jane: Oh, I don't want to **make waves.** They probably **would't take any notice** anyway.

Bob: Yes, I know what you mean - they seem a bit **way-out**.

Jane: It's not just the noise...Look at their place - it's such an **eyesore**. We just don't **hit it off**. I wish they were like Chris and Tom, on the other side. They're **terrific**! They've lived there for years and we've never had any problems. But these other people...Oh I don't know what to do. By the way, what are the new people next door to you like? Have you met them yet?

Bob: No I haven't... but they seem to be a bit **standoffish**. I've tried to say hello but they **give me the cold shoulder**. So I think they're **stuck up**, if you ask me.

Jane: Oh dear....well I suppose it's better than having a **nosy** person, like Mrs Jones, living next door.

Bob: Mrs Jones?

Jane: Yes... you know **the busybody** from number five. She knows everything that's **going on** in the street.... In fact she's probably watching us right now.

Bob: Yeah probably.

Jane: Oh well, it takes all kinds to make a world.

Now let's see what the underlined expressions mean - look at the next page.

CONVERSATION 2 - (explanation of everyday expressions)

Compare Conversation 1 with Conversation 2 - You will see that some of the words are different but the meaning is the same in both conversations. Find the underlined expressions in Conversation 1, then underline the words with the same meaning in Conversation 2. For example: <u>out of sorts</u> (Conversation 1) = <u>unhappy/unwell</u> (Conversation 2)

Bob: Hi Jane. How are you?

Jane: I'm feeling a bit <u>unhappy/unwell</u> this morning, Bob. I didn't sleep at all last night. The people next door were making a lot of noise again until very late at night. They don't care about anyone else. I'm very unhappy with the situation but I don't know what to do about it.

Bob: Why don't you tell them that you are displeased/upset with them.

Jane: Oh, I don't want to cause trouble. They probably wouldn't listen/act on what I say anyway.

Bob: Yes, I know what you mean - they seem a bit strange/unusual.

Jane: It's not just the noise...Look at their place - it's such an ugly thing/place to look at. We just don't like each other. I wish they were like Chris and Tom, on the other side. They're excellent! They've lived there for years and we've never had any problems. But these other people......Oh I don't know what to do. By the way, what are the new people next door to you like? Have you met them yet?

Bob: No, I haven't......but they seem to be a bit unfriendly. I've tried to say hello, but they deliberately ignore me. So I think they believe they are superior to me, if you ask me.

Jane: Oh dear........ well I suppose it's better than having a person who is always watching what other people are doing, like Mrs. Jones, living next door.

Bob: Mrs. Jones?

Jane: Yes....you know, the interfering person from number five. She knows everything that is happening in the street...In fact she's probably watching us right now.

Bob: Yes probably.

Jane: Oh well, it takes all kinds to make a world.

Important note:
The language used in Conversation 2 (above) may seem easier to understand when compared with Conversation 1. However, the 'everyday' expressions used in Conversation 1 are used extensively by speakers of English. Therefore it is beneficial to become familiar with the everyday expressions used by the speakers in **Conversation 1**.

◀◀ **Replay Conversation 1**
Listen to the conversation again and fill in the missing words. Don't worry about your spelling, as this exercise focuses on your listening skills - you can check your spelling later. (You may have to listen more than once.)

Bob: Hi Jane. How are you?

Jane: I'm feeling a bit _____ **of sorts** this morning, Bob. I **didn't sleep a** _____ last night. The people next door were making **a racket** again until _____ **hours**. They **couldn't care** _____ about anyone else. I'm **fed** ____ with the situation but I just don't know what to do about it.

Bob: Why don't you **give them a** _____ **of your mind**?

Jane: Oh, I don't want to **make** _____. They probably wouldn't _____ **any notice** anyway.

Bob: Yes. I know what you mean - They seem a bit _____ **out**.

Jane: It's not just the noise...Look at their place - it's such an **eyesore**. We just don't _____ **it off**. I wish they were like Chris and Tom, on the other side. They're **terrific**! They've lived there for years and we've never had any problems. But these other people…Oh I don't know what to do. By the way, what are the new people next door to you like? Have you met them yet?

Bob: No I haven't..... but they seem to be **a bit** _____ **offish**. I've tried to say hello but they **give me the** _____ **shoulder**. So I think they're **stuck** _____, if you ask me.

Jane: Oh dear...well I suppose it's better than having a _____ person like Mrs Jones living next door.

Bob: Mrs Jones?

Jane: Yes... you know **the busy** _____ from number five. She knows everything that's **going** ____ in the street..... In fact she's probably watching us right now.

Bob: Yeah, probably.

Jane: Oh well. It takes all kinds to make a world.

Now check your answers by comparing this page with
CONVERSATION 1.

◀◀ Replay Conversation 1
In order to become more familiar with these new everyday expressions:
1) Listen and tick the boxes ☑ next to the expressions as you hear them.
2) Write in the definitions you can remember. (One has been done as an example.)
   Check your answers with the reference list on page 124.

	Expression	Definition
☐	out of sorts...................................	*unhappy/unwell*
☐	didn't sleep a wink............................	_____
☐	a racket......................................	_____
☐	all hours.....................................	_____
☐	couldn't care less............................	_____
☐	fed up..	_____
☐	give (them) a piece of your mind..............	_____
☐	make waves....................................	_____
☐	wouldn't take any notice......................	_____
☐	way-out.......................................	_____
☐	eyesore.......................................	_____
☐	hit it off....................................	_____
☐	terrific......................................	_____
☐	standoffish...................................	_____
☐	give (me) the cold shoulder...................	_____
☐	stuck up......................................	_____
☐	nosy..	_____
☐	a busybody....................................	_____
☐	going on......................................	_____

LANGUAGE NOTES:

1. In the expression, 'They give *me* the cold shoulder' other pronouns (*us, them, him* etc.) can be used.
2. To '*make* a racket' means to make a noise (as in Conversation 1 of this unit), however, to be '*involved* in a 'racket' means to be involved in a dishonest business.
3. 'a busybody' refers to one person; 'busybod<u>ies</u>' refers to more than one person.

CROSSWORD - LANGUAGE REVISION

Complete the sentences, choosing from the expressions or words listed in the box below.
You can use the clues in brackets ( ) at the end of each sentence to help you.
Then complete the crossword using the everyday expressions you have written.
The first one has been done as an example.

sorts	hit it off	~~standoffish~~	all hours	eyesore	piece
stuck up	make waves	cold shoulder	fed up	nosy	busybodies

ACROSS

1) My boyfriend's parents aren't very friendly to me. They are ***standoffish*** towards me when I visit them. (unfriendly)

3) He felt *out of* _____ after hearing the terrible news. (unhappy/unwell)

5) Mrs Jones is very _____. She watches what everyone is doing from her window. (inquisitive)

7) I'm ____ ___ with my boring job but I don't know what to do. (very unhappy)

9) I'm very upset with Ann. I'm going to give her a _____ *of my mind* when I see her. (tell her I'm upset with her)

11) I wish the people next door would tidy their garden. It's an _____. (ugly place to look at)

DOWN

2) My in-laws are very _____ ___ . They think they are superior to me. (snobbish)

4) The cat from next door is always in my garden but I don't want to _____ _____ so I won't complain about it. (cause trouble)

6) Mrs Jones gives me the _____ _____ every time I try to say hello. She doesn't want to be friendly. (deliberately ignores)

8) The students in my class all ____ ___ ___ really well. Everyone is friendly. (like each other)

10) Last night, I stayed up till ___ _____ ,finishing my homework. (very late at night)

12) The people next door are _____. They're always trying to tell us what to do. (interfering people)

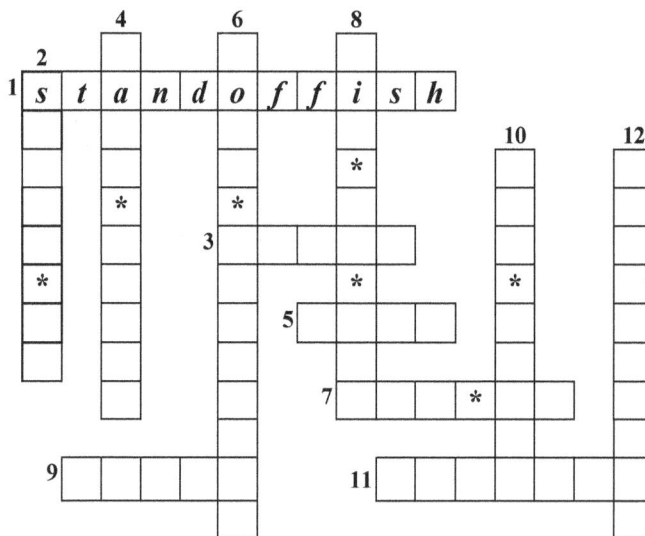

(Answers: page 112)

FOCUS ON SPOKEN LANGUAGE

A) Using pronouns

Pronouns (words such as *I, you, they, she, him, we, it, etc.*) are often used in English as a *substitute* for *previously mentioned names or things (nouns)*. To repeat the name continually sounds very unnatural.

For example, we say: 'Where is *Sam*? I told *him* to come as soon as possible. *He*'s in trouble.'
        (noun)   (pronoun)   (pronoun)

We *do not* say: 'Where is *Sam*? I told *Sam* to come as soon as possible. *Sam*'s in trouble.'
        (noun)   (noun)   (noun)

Sometimes the <u>same</u> pronoun is used in a conversation to refer to <u>different</u> people.
For example, in the excerpt from Conversation 1 below, the pronoun '**they**' refers to several different people. For example **'they'** may refer to **'the people next door who were making a racket'** or **'Chris and Tom, on the other side'** or **'the new people, next door to Bob'.**

- Read the conversation and decide who 'they' refers to in each of the underlined sentences, then do the exercise below.

Bob:	Hi Jane. How are you?
Jane:	I'm feeling a bit out of sorts this morning, Bob. I didn't sleep a wink last night. The **1)** people next door were making a racket again until all hours. *They* couldn't care less about anyone else. I'm fed up with the situation but I just don't know what to do about it.
Bob:	Why don't you give them a piece of your mind?
Jane:	Oh, I don't want to make waves. They probably wouldn't take any notice anyway. **2)**
Bob:	Yes, I know what you mean - *they* seem a bit way-out.
Jane:	It's not just the noise..... Look at their place - it's such an eyesore. We just don't hit it off. I wish **3)** **4)** they were like Chris and Tom, on the other side. *They*'re terrific! *They*'ve lived there for years and we've never had any problems. But these other people ....Oh I don't know what to do. By the way, what are the new people next door to you like? Have you met them yet? **5)** **6)**
Bob:	No I haven't...... but *they* seem to be a bit standoffish. I've tried to say hello but *they* give me the cold shoulder.

- **Write your answers on the correct lines below. One has been done as an example.**

1) *They* refers to 'the people next door who were making a racket'

2) *They* refers to_____

3) *They* refers to_____

4) *They* refers to_____

5) *They* refers to_____

6) *They* refers to_____

You can check your answers on page 112 .

B) Pronouns - pronunciation and spelling

In spoken language, pronouns are often followed by a contraction.
For example, *'he is'* becomes *he's*; *'they are'* becomes *they're*.
These pronouns are often confused with other words that have the same pronunciation.
Look at the **_underlined_** words in the following sentence from Conversation 1.

> Jane: …Look at **_their_** place - it's such an eyesore. We just don't hit it off. I wish they were like.
> Chris and Tom, on the other side. **_They're_** terrific!

If you listen to this sentence, you will see that '**_their_**' and '**_they're_**' are pronounced similarly.
However, they have different meanings: '**_their_**' shows possession; '**_they're_** ' is a contraction of '*they are*'.

The same problem can occur with other pronouns.
Look at the following sentences. The **bold** words in each sentence are pronounced the same.

- The dog has eaten **its** dinner and now **it's** sitting quietly in the corner.
  (**its** shows possession; **it's** = it is)

- **His** mother said **he's** very lazy. (**his** shows possession; **he's** = he is)
  Note: '**his**' is pronounced with a short vowel sound /hɪz/ whereas '**he's**' is pronounced with a long vowel sound /hiːz/, however, the correct usage of these words is often confused.

- **You're** clever because you always finish **your** homework first.
  (**you're** = you are; **your** shows possession)

- We **were** too late yesterday to see the movie so **we're** going to see it today.
  (**were** is a past plural verb; **we're** = we are)

B) Practice - pronunciation and spelling

Complete the following sentences, by choosing the correct word from the box and writing it in
the appropriate space. Answers, page 112.

it's	*its*	*their*	*they're*	*were*	*we're*	*he's*	*his*	*you're*	*your*

1) _____ very upset because we lost our camera when we _____ overseas last month.

2) _____ very happy that he's passed _____ driving test!

3) _____ much taller than _____ sister but she's older than you, isn't she?

4) The cat has eaten _____ dinner and now _____ sitting under the tree.

5) _____ coming by train because _____ car is being repaired.

C) Changing the topic during a conversation

In spoken English we use certain expressions when we want to change the topic of conversation or when something that is said reminds us of something else we want to ask or talk about. Some of these expressions are:

By the way,…
eg. 'It's very cold outside today, isn't it? *By the way*, I've ordered a new heater for the office. It was a very good price.'

While I think of it, …
eg. 'It's very cold outside today, isn't it? *While I think of it*, I've ordered a new heater for the office. It was a very good price.'

That reminds me,...
eg. 'It's very cold outside today, isn't it? *That reminds me*, I've ordered a new heater for the office. It was a very good price.'

Listen to Conversation 1 again. You will notice that Jane changes the topic of conversation from complaining about the people next door to her, to asking about the new people next door to Bob. Which expression does she use to introduce the new topic? Write the expression on the line below.

_____

(Answer: page 112)

D) Giving an opinion

In spoken English, we show that we are giving or expressing our opinion in several ways.
We can introduce our opinion by saying, '*In my opinion*, the price of petrol is unfair.'
               or 'The price of petrol is unfair, *in my opinion*.'

Another way to introduce our opinion is: '*If you ask me*, the price of petrol is unfair.'
               or 'The price of petrol is unfair, *if you ask me*.'

We also introduce an opinion by saying: '*As far as I'm concerned*, the price of petrol is unfair.'

Which of these expressions did Bob use when he was talking about his neighbours?
Check Conversation 1 and write your answer below.

_____

(Answer: page 112)

(Units 1 - 3)

This section reviews some of the expressions that were introduced in Units 1, 2, and 3 and gives you a chance to see what you have remembered.

- Look at the pictures on the opposite page and decide what the people are saying by choosing from the expressions below.

- Match each picture with an appropriate expression by writing the correct letter in the box next to each expression.

- For extra practice, you could write the appropriate expression in the space provided in the picture.

1) This is beyond me. I don't understand one word. ☐

2) Unfortunately poor eyesight runs in our family. ☐

3) It looks like we'll have to start from scratch again, my dear. ☐

4) I don't know why she is so stuck up. She thinks she is better than us. ☐

5) Look at Mrs Jones. She's such a busybody! ☐

6) Your work is terrific. I'm really happy with it. ☐

7) I knew I'd get the hang of it, if I stuck at it. ☐

8) You'll keep in touch, won't you? ☐

9) Well, it looks like we're all in the same boat! ☐

(Answers: page 112)

UNIT 4

TALKING ABOUT SHOPPING

Some people love shopping while others hate it. A person who loves shopping is sometimes jokingly called a 'shopaholic'. This means shopping has become a habit that they can't control. Do you know any shopaholics?

Listening for general understanding

Listen to this conversation between friends who are shopping. (Unit 4 on the audio recording.) The conversation contains colloquial or everyday expressions that will be explained later in the unit - so don't worry if you don't understand every word. This time you are only listening for general understanding of the topic. As you listen, tick the correct answers below. (There may be more than one correct answer.)

When you have finished you can check your answers on page 113.

1) What does Mari (first speaker) want to shop around for?

    a) a book

    b) a pair of shoes

    c) some furniture

2) Ingrid and Mari are having the conversation:

    a) before they start shopping

    b) after they have finished shopping

3) Ingrid and Mari:

    a) both enjoy shopping

    b) both hate shopping

4) What time do the friends have to finish shopping?

    a) twelve o' clock

    b) two o' clock

    c) two thirty

Now, we'll look at the everyday expressions used in the conversation – turn to the next page.

CONVERSATION 1 (with everyday expressions)

◀◀ **Replay Conversation 1**
Read this conversation as you listen to the audio recording. Do you know what the _underlined_ words mean? They are colloquial or 'everyday' expressions.

Mari: I'm **a bit broke** at the moment Ingrid, so I don't want to spend too much today, but I'd like to **shop around** for a pair of shoes that don't **cost an arm and a leg**.

Ingrid: Yeah, some shoes are **a rip-off** aren't they? We could **check out** the new shoe store next to the **deli**.

Mari: Oh, I think that store looks a bit **pricey** and I've heard they can be **pushy** in there too… but we can have a look. I want to **pick up** a few **bits and pieces** at the deli anyway. **What're you after**?

Ingrid: Well, I'm going to have **a spending spree**! I want to buy some new clothes for work and I was hoping you'd help me. You seem to have **the knack of** finding bargains.

Mari: OK, that'll be fun.

Ingrid: As you know, I often get **conned into** buying clothes that are far too expensive; and then **more often than not** I don't like them when I try them on again at home.

Mari: That's because you buy things **on the spur of the moment**. You see something and you buy it… or you let yourself get talked into it!*

Ingrid: I know. But in future I'm going to **mend my ways** and shop around like you.

Mari: OK. Well let's start at the shoe store. But remember I have to go at two thirty. You won't **get carried away** with your shopping and **lose track of** time, will you?

Ingrid: Don't worry, I won't! I have to go at two thirty as well.

*'To get talked into doing something' means 'to be persuaded to do something' (see Conversation 1, Unit 1)

Now let's see what the underlined expressions mean - look at the next page.

CONVERSATION 2 (explanation of everyday expressions)

Compare Conversation 1 with Conversation 2 - You will see that some of the words are different but the meaning is the same in both conversations. Find the underlined expressions in Conversation 1, then underline the words with the same meaning in Conversation 2. For example: <u>a bit broke</u> (Conversation 1) = <u>don't have much money</u> (Conversation 2)

Mari: I <u>don't have much money</u> at the moment Ingrid, so I don't want to spend too much today, but I'd like to visit a few shops to look for the best price for a pair of shoes that don't cost too much money.

Ingrid: Yeah, some shoes are over-priced aren't they? We could look at/investigate the new shoe store next to the delicatessen (the shop which sells cooked meat and cheese).

Mari: Oh, I think that store looks a bit expensive and I've heard they can be very persistent in there too… but we can have a look. I want to get/collect a few small items at the deli anyway. What are you looking for?

Ingrid: Well, I'm going to have an enjoyable time spending money. I want to buy some new clothes for work and I was hoping you'd help me. You seem to have the ability/skill of finding bargains.

Mari: OK, that'll be fun.

Ingrid: As you know, I often get persuaded/tricked into buying clothes that are far too expensive; and then usually/often I don't like them when I try them on again at home.

Mari: That's because you buy things on impulse. You see something and you buy it… or you let yourself get talked into it!

Ingrid: I know. But in future I'm going to reform/improve my habits and shop around like you.

Mari: OK. Well let's start at the shoe store. But remember I have to go at two thirty. You won't become too interested and involved with your shopping and forget about time, will you?

Ingrid: Don't worry, I won't! I have to go at two thirty as well.

Important note:
The language used in Conversation 2 (above) may seem easier to understand when compared with Conversation 1. However, the 'everyday' expressions used in Conversation 1 are used extensively by speakers of English. Therefore it is beneficial to become familiar with the everyday expressions used by the speakers in **Conversation 1**.

◄◄ **Replay Conversation 1**
Listen to the conversation again and fill in the missing words. You may need to listen more than once. (Don't worry about your spelling as this activity focuses on listening skills; you can check your spelling later.)

Mari: I'm **a bit _____** at the moment Ingrid, so I don't want to spend too much today, but I'd like to **shop around** for a pair of shoes that don't **cost an arm and a _____**.

Ingrid: Yeah, some shoes are **a _____** aren't they? We could **check _____** the new shoe store next to the **deli**.

Mari: Oh, I think that store looks a bit **pricey** and I've heard they can be **pushy** in there too …but we can have a look. I want to **pick up** a few **_____ and pieces** at the deli anyway. **What're you _____**?

Ingrid: Well, I'm going to have **a spending spree**! I want to buy some new clothes for work and I was hoping you'd help me. You seem to have **the _____ of** finding bargains.

Mari: OK, that'll be fun.

Ingrid: As you know, I often get **_____ into** buying clothes that are far too expensive; and then **more often than not** I don't like them when I try them on again at home.

Mari: That's because you buy things **on the _____ of the moment**. You see something and you buy it… or you let yourself get talked into it!

Ingrid: I know. But in future I'm going to **_____ my ways** and shop around like you.

Mari: OK. Well let's start at the shoe store. But remember I have to go at two thirty. You won't **get _____ away** with your shopping and **lose _____ of** time, will you?

Ingrid: Don't worry, I won't! I have to go at two thirty as well.

> Now check your answers by comparing this page with CONVERSATION 1.

◄◄ **Replay Conversation 1**

In order to become more familiar with these new everyday expressions:
1) **Listen and tick the boxes ☑ next to the expressions as you hear them.**
2) **Write in the definitions you can remember. (The first one has been done as an example.)**
   Check your answers with the reference list on page 125.

☐	a bit broke..................................	*to not have much money*
☐	shop around.................................	_____
☐	cost an arm and a leg......................	_____
☐	*a rip-off....................................	_____
☐	(to) check out..............................	_____
☐	the deli.....................................	_____
☐	pricey......................................	_____
☐	pushy......................................	_____
☐	pick up.....................................	_____
☐	bits and pieces.............................	_____
☐	What are you after?........................	_____
☐	a spending spree...........................	_____
☐	the knack of...............................	_____
☐	conned into................................	_____
☐	more often than not........................	_____
☐	on the spur of the moment..................	_____
☐	mend (my) ways...........................	_____
☐	get carried away...........................	_____
☐	lose track of...............................	_____

LANGUAGE NOTE:

The expression '**a rip-off**' is generally used singularly even when referring to plural nouns.
eg. The tickets were *a rip-off*. (The tickets were *overpriced*.)

The expression '**check out**' can have several meanings, depending on the context.
A *check out* (noun) means '*the payment counter in a supermarket*'.
To *check out* (verb) can mean to '*finalise departure at a hotel*'.
To *check out* (verb) can mean to '*look at/investigate*' (as used in Conversation 1 of this unit).

The expression '**pick up**' can have several meanings, depending on the context.
To '*pick up*' can mean '*improve in health*'. eg. He's *picked up* a lot today. (See Unit 5)
To '*pick up*' something can mean '*learn easily*'. eg. I *pick up* other languages very quickly.
To '*pick up*' (someone) can mean '*to meet someone casually*' (possibly for sexual purposes).
To '*pick up*' (something or someone) can mean collect/get. eg. I *pick up* my son from school
at three o' clock each day.

(See the note on the word order of phrasal verbs, in Unit 9, Part 6D)

CROSSWORD - LANGUAGE REVISION

Complete the sentences, choosing from the expressions or words listed below. You can use the clues in brackets ( ) at the end of each sentence to help you.
Then complete the crossword using the everyday expressions you have written.
The first one has been done as an example.

mend my ways	~~spur of the moment~~	conned into	arm and a leg	deli
pick up pushy	the knack of	spending spree	rip-off	shop around

ACROSS

1) He decided on the _____ ___ ____ _____ to book a holiday to Rome. (on impulse)
3) I _____ ___ my son from school at three o' clock each day. (collect/get)
5) I think she was _____ _____ buying that car. It was too expensive.(persuaded/tricked)
7) The shop assistant was so _____! I had to say, 'No, I'm not interested.' three times! (persistent)
9) I'm going to _____ _____ before I make a decision on the type of car to buy. (look for the best price)
11) Houses in this area cost an _____ _____ __ _____. (a lot of money/too much money)

DOWN

2) I had a _____ _____ with my credit card but now I have to pay for it! (an enjoyable time spending money)
4) Look at the price of this car! It's a ____ ___! (overpriced)
6) I haven't saved any money this year. But I'm going to _____ __ _____ next year. (reform/improve my habits)
8) He is a great entertainer. He has ____ _____ ___ making people laugh. (the ability/skill of)
10) Could you go to the _____ for me and buy some cheese? (shop that sells cooked meat and cheese)

(Answers: page 113)

FOCUS ON SPOKEN LANGUAGE

A) Question tags - revision

In Unit 2, we examined the use of *question tags* in conversational language. For example,
"It's hot today, *isn't it?*" (The ending, *"isn't it?"* is called the question tag).

Remember the pattern!
If the first part of the sentence has a *positive* verb, the question tag is *negative*.
If the first part of the sentence has a *negative* verb, the question tag is *positive.*
When the speaker is using this pattern to get confirmation, the listener agrees with the statement
in the first part of the sentence. Look at the following example:

Statement	Question tag	Short Reply
'Cooler weather *will* be here soon,	won't it?'	'Yes, it sure *will*.'
'The shop *was*n't busy today,	was it?'	'No, it *wasn't*.'

Practice

Find two sentences in Conversation 1 with question tags. Write them under the correct section
below. (There is no reply to the first statement.)

Statement	Question tag	Short reply
1)		_____
2)		

(Answers: page 113)

B) Using intonation to communicate meaning

Intonation refers to the way the voice goes up and down in pitch when we are speaking.
In English, speakers use intonation in various ways to convey meaning.

Intonation with question tags
When using question tags to be conversational and when seeking agreement, the speaker's
intonation falls on the question tag.

◀◀**Replay Conversation 1**

Listen to the speakers using question tags with falling intonation when they expect the listener to confirm or agree with what they have said.

'Some shoes are a rip-off, aren't they?'

'You won't get carried away with your shopping and lose track of time, will you?'

Note that if a speaker, using a tag question, is **unsure** of the answer, the intonation pattern will generally **rise** at the end, indicating that it is a real question.

C) Developing awareness of 'weak forms' in spoken English

In Unit One you learnt that in English, speakers **stress** words that are considered most **important** to the message. These words are given more emphasis than the other words in the message.

eg. The **books** are on the **desk**.

Words that do *not* carry the main message of the speaker are spoken quickly and softly; they are weak or unstressed. The weak, unstressed sound of English is shown in dictionaries as the symbol ə. This sound is the most frequently used sound in the major varieties of English. (ie. North American, Australian and British English)

Some very common words in English, such as '*a*', '*for*', '*at*', '*the*', '*to*', '*an*', '*and* ', '*of*' are often pronounced with a weak pronunciation. When these words are pronounced with a weak sound, they are referred to as **weak forms** (meaning *unstressed words*), containing the sound /ə/.

Practice

Read the first few lines of Conversation 1 below and decide which words are missing.
Choose from the words shown in the box.

	to	at	the	a	for	and	an	of

Mari: I'm _ bit broke __ _____ moment Ingrid, so I don't want ___ spend too much today but I'd like ___ shop around ____ __ pair __ shoes that don't cost ___ arm ____ __ leg.

◀◀**Replay Conversation 1**

Listen to the first two lines of Conversation 1 and check your answers.
As you listen, notice the weak pronunciation of the words you have written.

You can also check your answers on page 113.

D) The linking of words in connected speech

In **written** English, words are seen separately, with spaces between them on a page. However, in **spoken** language, the words of a fluent speaker are not usually heard as separate, distinct words but are linked together into groups of words.

When speaking in a natural, fluent, conversational way, English speakers (including educated speakers) link words together to help the smooth flow of speech. This is called **connected speech**. Below are some examples of the ways in which words are linked in connected speech.

Linking of consonant sound to vowel sound

- In spoken English, speakers usually link words that <u>end in a consonant sound</u> with a <u>following word that begins with a vowel sound</u>. Look at the example from the first line of Conversation 1. The linked sounds are shown with the symbol ‿ in between the linked words.

$$\text{eg. I'm} \smile \text{a bit broke} \smile \text{at the moment} \smile \text{Ingrid}$$

Note that in the word 'broke', the final <u>sound</u> is the consonant sound /k/, as the letter 'e' is not pronounced.; it is silent.

Linking of consonant sound to consonant sound

- Linking also occurs between words when the *same* consonant *sound* ends one word and begins the next word. For example, the 't' sound in the words 'nex<u>t to</u>' is linked. The <u>linking sound</u> is usually pronounced only *once*, but a little longer than usual. Look at the example from the first line of Conversation:

$$\text{eg. 'We could check out the new shoe store next} \smile \text{to the deli.'}$$

Deleting of sounds in fast connected speech

- In fast, connected speech some sounds may be deleted by the speaker. For example, the sound /t/ may be deleted between the words 'want to', making the pronunciation of 'want to' sound like 'wǝnnǝ '. (Note: the symbol ǝ represents a very short, weak sound.)

You will hear an example of this in the first sentence of Conversation 1.

eg. '…I don't *want to* spend too much today…'

You will listen to and read the examples of linking and deletion of words in Conversation 1 when you turn to the next page.

◀◀ **Replay Conversation 1**
   Listen to the examples of linking between words in the first few lines of Conversation 1.

Mari: I'm‿a bit broke‿at the moment‿Ingrid, so I don't *wɐnnə* want to spend too much today

   but‿I'd like to shop‿around for‿a pair‿of shoes that don't cost‿an‿arm‿and‿a

   leg.

Ingrid: Yeah, some shoes‿are‿a rip-off‿aren't they? We could check‿out the new shoe

   store next‿to the deli.

(Note that in the word 'are', the final sound is the consonant sound /r/, as the letter 'e' is not pronounced.)

(See page 53 for a summary on 'Connected Speech'.)

Note: It is not completely necessary for learners of English to link words in this way to be
   understood by others. It is important however, for students to be *aware* of this feature
   of spoken language in order *to understand* the connected speech of native English speakers
   and to realise that the use of these features helps the smooth flow of speech.

Reference page
Understanding Connected Speech

When speaking in a natural, fluent, conversational way, English speakers (including educated speakers) contract and link words to help the smooth flow of speech.

Some ways words are linked in connected speech:

1) Contracted words are linked to the word before it.

    eg.   The <u>book is</u> here.   ➡   The <u>book's</u> here.

          The <u>job will</u> be finished soon. ➡ The <u>job'll</u> be finished soon.

    See Unit 1, Part 6B for more information on contractions.

2) Unstressed words (called weak forms) are reduced (spoken quickly).
    For example, words like *'a', 'an', 'of.'*

    / ə /   /ə/
    <u>A</u> cup‿<u>of</u> tea. *See Unit 4, Part 6C for more information on 'weak forms'.*

3) Words ending with a <u>consonant</u> sound and followed by words starting with a <u>vowel</u> sound are usually linked.

               ➡
    eg. loo<u>k</u> <u>o</u>ut   lookout.
                   ‿

4) Words ending with a <u>consonant</u> sound are usually linked to words starting with the <u>same consonant sound</u>. The sound is pronounced only once, but a little longer.

               ➡
    eg. bu<u>s</u> <u>s</u>top   busstop
                   ‿

    See Unit 4, Part 6D for more information on 'linking'.

5) In fast, connected speech some sounds may be deleted.
    For example, the sounds /d/ and /h/ are often deleted in unstressed words.

                  /əv/   /ən/
    eg. Many books ha̶ve been written about health an̶d happiness

6) Words ending with a <u>vowel</u> sound which are followed by words starting with a <u>vowel</u> sound can be linked with a 'linking sound'. For example, when a word which ends with /uː/ or /ʊ/ is followed by a word beginning with a vowel sound, speakers often link the words with the sound /w/ in fluent speech. Eg. Who‿else? 'There's two‿in the queue.'
                                   /w/   /w/

You can learn more about the pronunciation of English in the book,
'Understanding English Pronunciation – an integrated practice course'.
See details on the final page of this book.

UNIT 5

TALKING ABOUT HEALTH AND SICKNESS

Before you listen to a conversation between a doctor and patient (Unit 5 of the audio recording), check the meaning of the following words in a dictionary if you are not familiar with their meaning.

prescription	examination	symptoms	virus

Write the word next to its correct meaning on the lines below: (Answers: page 113)

• a sickness caused by a germ/micro-organism _____

• signs or changes to the health of a person _____

• a doctor's written instruction for the use of medicine _____

• a careful inspection _____

Listening for general understanding

Listen to the conversation between a doctor and patient. The conversation contains colloquial or 'everyday' expressions which will be explained later in the unit - so don't worry if you don't understand every word. This time you are only listening for a general understanding of the topic. As you listen, tick the correct answer below.
(There may be more than one correct answer) Answers: page 113.

1) Mrs Smith is visiting the doctor because:

a) her daughter is sick

b) she is pregnant

c) her son is sick

d) she feels unwell

2) One of Mrs Smith's symptoms is:

a) a backache

b) a headache

c) vomiting

3) The doctor suggests that she should:

a) have an operation

b) have a few days off work

c) take some headache tablets

Now, we'll look at the everyday expressions used in the conversation – turn to the next page.

CONVERSATION 1 (with everyday expressions)

◀◀ **Replay Conversation 1**
Read this conversation as you listen to the audio recording. Do you know what the
underlined **words mean? They are colloquial or 'everyday' expressions.**

Doctor:	What seems to be the problem, Mrs Smith?
Mrs Smith:	Well actually, it's my son. He's had a fever since Wednesday and he's been **throwing up**. He's **picked up** a bit today but he's still **under the weather**.
Doctor:	Mm. He could have the **bug** that's going around. **Pop** him on the table and I'll give him **a check up**. Has he complained about a sore **tummy**?
Mrs Smith:	He did yesterday - not so much today.
Doctor:	Mm... alright, well just **keep an eye on** him. I'll give you a prescription for some medicine but I think he's **on the mend**. Is there anything else?
Mrs Smith:	Yes. I'd like you to **take a look at** me while I'm here. I think I'm **coming down with something**. Usually I'm **as fit as a fiddle** but the last couple of days I've been feeling really **off**.
Doctor:	Mm. It could be the same **bug**.... Any other symptoms?
Mrs Smith:	Yes, I feel really **run-down** and I've had a **splitting headache**.
Doctor:	And when did these symptoms **come on**?
Mrs Smith	About five days ago... but I've been having bad headaches for a while now.
Doctor:	Mm. Have you been **overdoing it** lately? Are you worrying about something?
Mrs Smith:	I suppose I am. I've been **pretty uptight** lately about work at the office.
Doctor:	Well, first of all, I think you need a few days off work to **take it easy**. If the problem doesn't **clear up** in a few days we'll run some tests and see what we **come up with**.
Mrs Smith:	OK. Thank you Doctor.
Doctor:	Give me a call......

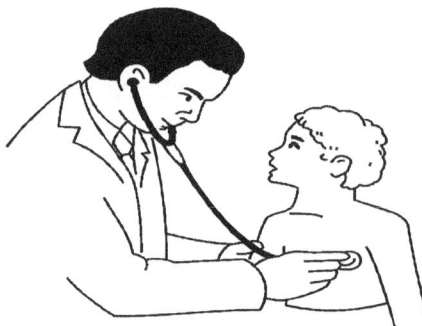

Now let's see what the underlined expressions mean - look at the next page.

CONVERSATION 2 (explanation of everyday expressions)

Compare Conversation 1 with Conversation 2 - You will see that some of the words are different but the meaning is the same in both conversations. Find the underlined expressions in Conversation 1, then underline the words with the same meaning in Conversation 2. For example: throwing up (Conversation 1) = vomiting (Conversation 2)

Doctor:	What seems to be the problem, Mrs Smith?
Mrs Smith:	Well actually, it's my son. He's had a fever since Wednesday and he's been vomiting. He's improved a bit today but he's still unwell/sick.
Doctor:	Mm. He could have the virus that's going around. Put him on the table and I'll give him an examination. Has he complained about a sore stomach?
Mrs Smith:	He did yesterday - not so much today.
Doctor:	Mm… alright, well just keep a careful watch on him. I'll give you a prescription for some medicine but I think he's improving (in health). Is there anything else?
Mrs Smith:	Yes. I'd like you to examine me while I'm here. I think I'm getting a sickness. Usually I'm very healthy but the last couple of days I've been feeling really unwell.
Doctor:	Mm. It could be the same virus.... Any other symptoms?
Mrs Smith:	Yes, I feel really unwell/tired and I've had a very bad headache.
Doctor:	And when did these symptoms begin?
Mrs Smith:	About five days ago.... but I've been having bad headaches for a while now.
Doctor:	Mm. Have you been working too hard lately? Are you worrying about something?
Mrs Smith:	I suppose I am. I've been quite anxious lately about work at the office.
Doctor:	Well, first of all, I think you need a few days off work to relax. If the problem doesn't become better in a few days we'll run some tests and see what we find/discover.
Mrs Smith:	OK. Thank you Doctor.
Doctor:	Give me a call……

Important note:
The language used in Conversation 2 (above) may seem easier to understand when compared with Conversation 1. However, the 'everyday' expressions used in Conversation 1 are used extensively by speakers of English. Therefore it is beneficial to become familiar with the everyday expressions used by the speakers in **Conversation 1**.

◄◄ **Replay Conversation 1**
Listen to the conversation again and fill in the missing words. You may have to listen more than once. Don't worry about your spelling as this exercise focuses on listening skills - you can check your spelling later.

Doctor: What seems to be the problem, Mrs Smith?

Mrs Smith: Well actually, it's my son. He's had a fever since Wednesday and he's been

_____ **up**. He's **picked** _____ a bit today but he's still _____ **the weather**.

Doctor: Mm. He could have the _____ that's going around. **Pop** him on the table and I'll

give him **a check** _____. Has he complained about a sore **tummy**?

Mrs Smith: He did yesterday - not so much today.

Doctor: Mm… alright, well just **keep an** _____ **on** him. I'll give you a prescription for

some medicine but I think he's **on the** _____. Is there anything else?

Mrs Smith: Yes. I'd like you to **take a** _____ **at** me while I'm here. I think I'm **coming**

_____ **with something**. Usually I'm **as** _____ **as a fiddle** but the last couple

of days I've been feeling really _____.

Doctor: Mm. It could be the same **bug**... Any other symptoms?

Mrs Smith: Yes, I feel really _____ **down** and I've had a _____ **headache**.

Doctor: And when did these symptoms **come** _____?

Mrs Smith: About five days ago.... but I've been having bad headaches for a while now.

Doctor: Mm. Have you been _____ **doing it** lately? Are you worrying about

something?

Mrs Smith: I suppose I am. I've been **pretty** _____ **tight** lately about work at the office.

Doctor: Well first of all, I think you need a few days off work to **take it** _____.

If the problem doesn't _____ **up** in a few days we'll run some tests and

see what we **come** _____ **with**.

Mrs Smith: OK. Thank you Doctor.

Doctor: Give me a call……

Now check your answers by comparing this page with
CONVERSATION 1.

◀◀ Replay Conversation 1
In order to become more familiar with these new everyday expressions:
1) Listen and tick the boxes ☑ next to the expressions as you hear them.
2) Write the definitions you can remember on the line provided.
   (One has been done as an example.) Check your answers with the reference list on page 126.

☐ throwing up.. *vomiting* _____

☐ picked up.. _____

☐ under the weather.. _____

☐ a/the bug .... _____

☐ pop.. _____

☐ a check-up .... _____

☐ tummy.. _____

☐ keep an eye on.. _____

☐ on the mend.. _____

☐ take a look at.. _____

☐ coming down with (something).. _____

☐ fit as a fiddle.. _____

☐ off.. _____

☐ run-down.. _____

☐ a splitting headache.. _____

☐ come on.. _____

☐ overdoing it.. _____

☐ pretty uptight.. _____

☐ take it easy.. _____

☐ clear up.. _____

☐ come up with.. _____

LANGUAGE NOTE:
- The expression *'come on'* can mean 'begin/start' as in: 'When did the symptoms *come on*?'
- *Come on!* is also used as to tell someone to hurry. eg. *'Come on!* Everyone's waiting!'
- The expression *'to come on to' someone* means 'to show interest in someone in a sexual way'

CROSSWORD – VOCABULARY REVISION

Complete the sentences, using the everyday expressions that have been listed below. You can use the clues in brackets ( ) at the end of each sentence to help you. Then complete the crossword using the everyday expressions you have written. The first one has been done as an example.

run-down	throw up	~~clear up~~	come up with	on the mend	come down with
pick up	fit as a fiddle	keep an eye on	overdoing it	under the weather	

ACROSS

1) Did your headache ***clear up*** before the exam started? (become better)

3) I feel _____ _____ today. (tired/unwell)

5) I feel sick in the stomach. I think I'm going to _____ ____. (vomit)

7) If he tries very hard, he will _____ ___ _____ the answer. (find/discover)

9) I felt terrible yesterday but I'm ____ ____ _____ now. (improving in health)

11) I've been _____ ___ at work. I think I need a relaxing holiday. (working too hard)

DOWN

2) He's been _____ _____ _____ for a week. He should go to the doctor. (unwell/sick)

4) Everyone at the office has the flu. I hope I don't _____ _____ _____ it too. (get sick)

6) If you take your medicine, you will _____ ___ in a few days. (improve in health)

8) He never gets sick. He's as _____ ___ ___ _____. (very healthy)

10) Could you _____ ___ _____ __ the baby while I go shopping? (keep a careful watch)

(Answers: page 114)

FOCUS ON SPOKEN LANGUAGE

A) Some intonation patterns of English

As you learnt in Unit 4, intonation refers to the way the voice goes up and down in pitch when we are speaking. In English, speakers use intonation in various ways to convey meaning.

As intonation is always related to the context in which it is used, it is *not* possible to give a 'rule' that applies in every situation. However, some general guidelines are given below with examples.

- Questions beginning with 'Wh' words, **When, Where, Why, What**, generally end with *falling intonation*. When speakers use this type of question, they are usually asking for an explanation or seeking new information.

- Statements/answers generally end with a *falling intonation*.
  Look at the following examples from Conversation 1. Notice the intonation patterns.

Doctor:	What seems to be the problem, Mrs Smith?
Mrs Smith:	Well actually, it's my son. He's had a fever since Wednesday...

- Questions which begin: **Is, Are, Have, Has**, generally require an answer meaning, 'yes' or 'no'. (However, the answer often includes more than 'yes' or 'no').

  These type of questions usually end with a *rising intonation*.

Doctor:	Has he complained about a sore tummy?

Practice

Look at the following section from Conversation 1. Using the patterns shown in the examples above, mark the probable intonation at the end of the questions and answers. Then listen to the audio recording of Conversation 1 of this unit to check your answers.

Doctor:	And when did these symptoms come on?
Mrs. Smith:	About five days ago.... but I've been having bad headaches for a while now.
Doctor:	Mm. Have you been overdoing it lately? Are you worrying about something?
Mrs Smith:	I suppose I am. I've been pretty uptight lately about work at the office.

(You can also check your answers on page 114).

Remember:
While the patterns described above apply in most cases, there can be variation depending on the speaker and the situation. It is therefore *not* possible to give a 'rule' that will apply in <u>every</u> situation.

B) Incomplete sentences in spoken language

In conversational speech, speakers do not always use complete sentences. In fact words are often left out, if the meaning is clear without using a complete sentence. This aspect of language is referred to in language grammar books as '*ellipsis*'.

For example:

Complete sentence	**Informal spoken language**
I will see you soon.	See you soon.
Are you coming?	Coming?

In Conversation 1, when the doctor asked: 'Any other symptoms?', he did not use a complete question. A complete question would be:

'*Do you have* any other symptoms?'

or

'*Are there* any other symptoms?'

Look at the following section from Conversation 1. Mrs Smith does not use a complete sentence when replying to the doctor's question. Finish her incomplete reply to make a complete sentence.

Doctor: Mm. Have you been overdoing it lately? Are you worrying about something?
Mrs Smith: I suppose I am _____

You can check your answer on page 114.

C) Phrasal verbs

In English it is common to use words such as 'up', 'in', 'on', after verbs to express a variety of meanings. For example, 'come in' is another way of saying 'enter'. These 'two word verbs' are called *phrasal verbs*.

Generally these 'two word' verbs produce a different meaning when the words are used together, to the meaning of the two words when they are used separately. For example, the words 'turn' and 'up' have a completely different meaning when used together as the verb, 'turn up', which means 'arrive/attend'. As there are many phrasal verbs in English, students should try to learn the meaning of each expression as it is encountered in different contexts.

Look at the following sentences used in Conversation 1 that contain phrasal verbs.
Underline the phrasal verbs and write the meaning of the phrasal verb on the lines provided.
(You can check your answers on page 114.)

1) He's picked up a lot today.   _____

2) And when did these symptoms come on?   _____

3) If the problem doesn't clear up in a few days we'll run some tests.   _____

For more information on phrasal verbs, see Unit 9, Part 6.

D) Stages in a medical consultation

During a medical consultation, the doctor usually asks questions about symptoms to decide what the problem may be. There are usually certain stages in a consultation, after the initial greeting. For example:

1) The doctor asks about the problem.
2) The patient talks about the symptoms (and answers the doctor's questions.)
3) The doctor examines the patient (and asks further questions.)
4) The doctor suggests what he/she thinks the problem may be.
5) The doctor suggests some treatment or further tests.
6) Closing of consultation.

Of course, **not all** consultations are **exactly** the same. Sometimes the doctor suggests what the problem might be **before** he/she examines the patient (or he/she may not need to examine the patient.) Look at Conversation 1 again (below) and write the number of the stage next to each section of the consultation. In this consultation, the doctor has **two** patients, Mrs Smith and her son, so some stages will occur more than once. Some sections have been numbered for you.

When you have finished, you can check your answers on page 115.

Doctor:	What seems to be the problem, Mrs Smith?	
Mrs. Smith:	Well actually, it's my son. He's had a fever since Wednesday and he's been *throwing up*. He's *picked up* a bit today but he's still *under the weather*.	
Doctor:	Mm. He could have the *bug* that's going around.	
	Pop him on the table and I'll give him *a check up*. Has he complained about a sore *tummy?*	3
Mrs. Smith:	He did yesterday - not so much today.	2
Doctor:	Mm...alright, well just *keep an eye on* him. I'll give you a prescription for some medicine but I think he's *on the mend*.	
	Is there anything else?	1
Mrs. Smith:	Yes. I'd like you to you *take a look at* me while I'm here. I think I'm coming *down with something*. Usually I'm *as fit as a fiddle* but the last couple of days I've been feeling really *off*.	
Doctor:	Mm. It could be the same bug....	
	Any other symptoms?	
Mrs. Smith:	Yes. I feel really *run down* and I've had *a splitting headache*.	
Doctor:	And when did these symptoms *come on?*	
Mrs. Smith:	About five days ago.... but I've been having bad headaches for a while now.	
Doctor:	Mm. Have you been *overdoing it* lately? Are you worrying about something?	
Mrs. Smith:	I suppose I am. I've been *pretty uptight* lately about work at the office.	
Doctor:	Well, first of all, I think you need a few days off work to *take it easy*. If the problem doesn't *clear up* in a few days we'll run some tests and see what we *come up with*.	
Mrs. Smith:	OK. Thank you Doctor.	
Doctor:	Give me a call......	6

UNIT 6

WORRYING ABOUT MONEY

How are we going to make ends meet this month?

There is an expression in English that says, 'Money doesn't go very far.' What do you think this means? In English we also say: 'Money doesn't grow on trees!' Do you have similar expressions about money in your first language?

In modern society, it is becoming a common practice for people to use 'plastic money' or credit cards to pay for the things they need or want. Do you think credit cards are a good idea?

Listening for general understanding

Listen to this conversation about money. (Unit 6 on the audio recording.) The conversation contains 'everyday' expressions which will be explained later in the unit - so don't worry if you don't understand every word. This time you are only listening for general understanding of the topic. As you listen, tick the correct answers below. (There may be more than one correct answer.) When you have finished you can check you answers on page 115.

---

1) Where is the conversation taking place?

    a) at work

    b) at home

    c) at the bank

2) What is the topic of conversation?

    a) household bills

    b) a bank account

    c) a tax form

3) During the conversation the speakers:

    a) have different opinions.

    b) have similar opinions.

Now, we'll look at the everyday expressions used in the conversation – turn to the next page.

CONVERSATION 1 (with everyday expressions)

◄◄ **Replay Conversation 1**
Read this conversation as you listen to the audio recording. Do you know what the
underlined **expressions mean? They are colloquial or 'everyday' expressions.**

Husband: Oh no, look at this phone bill! It's **gone through the roof** this time. Oh, I don't know.
                    We just don't seem to be able to **get ahead**.

Wife: Mm. I know what you mean. I can't **figure out** where all the money goes.
                    We always seem to be **forking out** for one bill or another. Maybe we'd better
                    sit down and **work out** a budget.

Husband: Yeah OK. **It's got me beat** though. Jim at work earns the same as me, yet they
                    seem to be pretty **well off**. They **splurged** on an expensive holiday last month and
                    here we are - we **can't make ends meet**.

Wife: They may seem to be well off but maybe they use plastic money. They may really
                    be **up to their ears** in debt, **for all we know**.

Husband: Mm maybe, **who knows**. I'd be happy if we could just **get by** and have a bit
                    spare to **put away** each week to **build a nest egg** - you know, **something to**
                    fall back on if something unexpected happens.

Wife: Mm. I know what you mean. I'm sick of **being flat broke** all the time too. We'll
                    have to talk to the kids about **going easy on** their phone calls in future.

Husband: Well, better still, we could ask them to **chip in** for the phone bill seeing they're the
                    ones who are on the phone for hours, **chatting** to their friends… And they're both
                    working part-time now.

Wife: Mm. That sounds fair enough to me. We could talk to them about it tonight.

Now let's see what the underlined expressions mean - look at the next page.

CONVERSATION 2 (explanation of everyday expressions)

Compare Conversation 1 with Conversation 2 - **You will see that some of the words are different but the meaning is the same in both conversations. Find the underlined expressions in Conversation 1, then underline the words with the same meaning in Conversation 2.**
For example: *gone through the roof* (Conversation 1) = *reached an very high price* (Conversation 2)

Husband: Oh no, look at this phone bill! It's <u>reached an extreme/very high price</u> this time. Oh I don't know. We just don't seem to be able to progress financially.

Wife: Mm. I know what you mean. I can't understand where all the money goes. We always seem to be unwillingly/reluctantly paying for one bill or another. Maybe we'd better sit down and plan the details of a budget.

Husband: Yes OK. I don't understand though. Jim at work earns the same as me, yet they seem to be pretty wealthy. They spent a lot of money on an expensive holiday last month, and here we are - we aren't able to pay our expenses.

Wife: They may seem to be well off but maybe they use plastic money. They may really be deeply (involved) in debt, we don't really know.

Husband: Mm maybe, I don't know the answer to that. I'd be happy if we could just manage our situation without difficulty and have a bit spare to save each week to get/have some savings for the future - you know something available as a reserve for future use if something unexpected happens.

Wife: Mm. I know what you mean. I'm sick of having no money all the time too. We'll have to talk to the children about using less/spending less (time) on their phone calls in future.

Husband: Well, better still, we could ask them to contribute some money for the phone bill seeing they're the ones who are on the phone for hours, talking informally to their friends… And they're both working part-time now.

Wife: Mm. That sounds fair enough to me. We could talk to them about it tonight.

Important note:
The language used in Conversation 2 (above) may seem easier to understand when compared with Conversation 1. However, the 'everyday' expressions used in Conversation 1 are used extensively by speakers of English. Therefore it is beneficial to become familiar with the everyday expressions used by the speakers in **Conversation 1.**

◄◄ **Replay Conversation 1**
Listen to the conversation again and fill in the missing words. You may have to listen more than once. (Don't worry about your spelling as this exercise focuses on listening skills - you can check your spelling later.)

Husband: Oh no, look at this phone bill! It's **gone through the** _____ this time. Oh, I don't know. We just don't seem to be able to **get ahead**.

Wife: Mm. I know what you mean. I can't **figure** _____ where all the money goes. We always seem to be **forking** _____ for one bill or another. Maybe we'd better sit down and _____ **out** a budget.

Husband: Yeah OK. **It's got me** _____ though. Jim at work earns the same as me, yet they seem to be pretty _____ **off**. They **splurged** on an expensive holiday last month and here we are - we **can't make** _____ **meet**.

Wife They may seem to be well off but maybe they use plastic money. They may really be **up to their** _____ in debt, **for all we know**.

Husband: Mm maybe, _____ **knows**. I'd be happy if we could just **get by** and have a bit spare to _____ **away** each week to **build a nest** _____ - you know, **something to fall back on** if something unexpected happens.

Wife: Mm. I know what you mean. I'm sick of **being flat** _____ all the time too. We'll have to talk to the kids about **going** _____ **on** their phone calls in future.

Husband: Well, better still, we could ask them to **chip** _____ for the phone bill seeing they're the ones who are on the phone for hours, _____ to their friends… And they're both working part-time now.

Wife: Mm, that sounds fair enough to me. We could talk to them about it tonight.

Now check your answers by checking this page with
CONVERSATION 1.

◀◀**Replay Conversation 1**
In order to become more familiar with these new everyday expressions:
1) **Listen and tick the boxes** ☑ **next to the expressions as you hear them.**
2) **Write in the definitions you can remember. (One has been done as an example.)**
   Check your answers with the reference list on page 127.

☐	gone through the roof..................	*reached a very high price*
☐	to get ahead	
☐	figure out	
☐	forking out ....……	
☐	work out	
☐	It's got me beat	
☐	well off	
☐	splurged...	
☐	can't make ends meet..................	
☐	up to (their) ears....................	
☐	for all we know....................	
☐	who knows..............................	
☐	get by...................................……	
☐	to put away (money)..................	
☐	build a nest egg..........................	
☐	something to fall back on.............	
☐	flat broke..................................	
☐	go easy on (something)............……	
☐	chip in......................................	
☐	chatting............................……	

LANGUAGE NOTE:

The expression, *'to go easy on (something)'* means to use sparingly, not use too much of (something). For example: *'Go easy on the milk, there's not much left.'* means *'Don't use too much milk, there's not much left.'*

The expression, *'to be up to my ears in (something)'* means *'to be deeply involved in something'* and usually refers to something unpleasant. eg. *'I'm up to my ears in work'*
The expression, *'I'm up to my eyes (or eyeballs) in* work' has the same meaning.

CROSSWORD - LANGUAGE REVISION

Complete the sentences, choosing from the everyday expressions which are listed in the box below. You can use the clues in brackets ( ) at the end of each sentence to help you. Then complete the crossword using the everyday expressions you have written. The first one has been done as an example.

fork out	through the roof	nest egg	chip in	~~fall back on~~	up to our ears
make ends meet	get by	put away	go easy on	who knows	broke

ACROSS

1) Take some extra travellers cheques in case you need something to ***fall back on***. (a reserve for future use)

3) The price of air travel has gone _____ _____ _____ in the past year. (reached an extreme/very high price)

5) 'Which team do you think will win the game?' 'Oh, _____ _____!' (I don't know.)

7) I _____ ___ on a small income. I have a strict budget and I'm careful with money (manage)

9) We've been ___ ___ ___ _____ in debt since I lost my job last year. (deeply involved in debt)

11) I need to get a better job. I can't _____ _____ _____ on my present salary. (pay my expenses)

DOWN

2) I have a small _____ _____ that I'm keeping for a nice holiday when I retire. (money saved)

4) Would you like to _____ ___ for Sue's wedding present? We're buying a lamp. (contribute)

6) I can't lend you any money. I'm _____ too! (don't have any money)

8) If we _____ _____ a small amount of money each week, we'd soon have enough to buy a small car. (saved)

10) If you _____ ____ for your son's speeding fines every time, he won't learn! (pay reluctantly)

12) ____ _____ ___ the milk. I will need some later! (use less of)

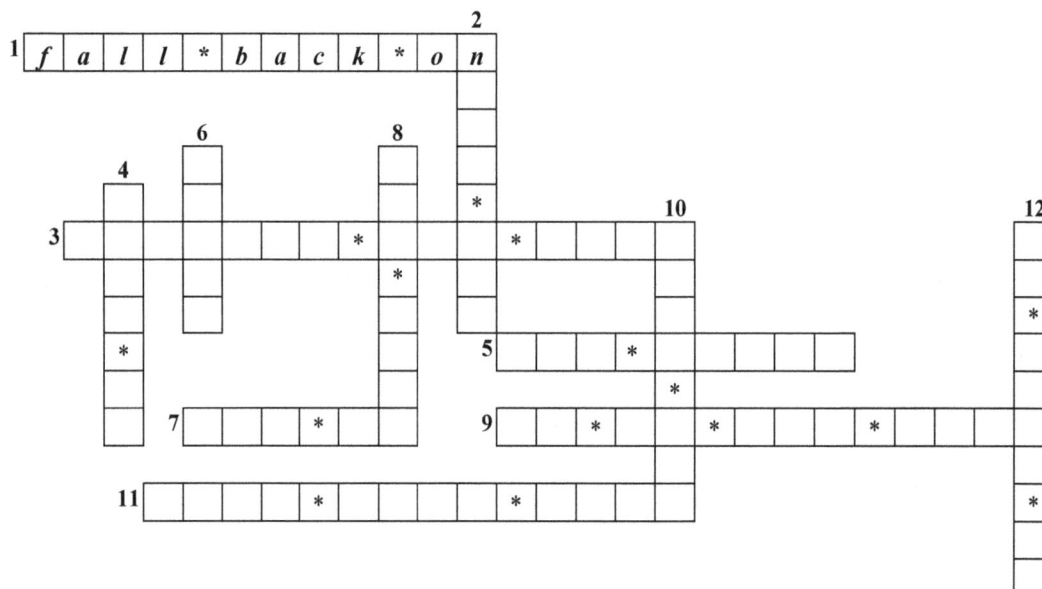

(Answers: page 115)

FOCUS ON SPOKEN LANGUAGE

A) Giving feedback

When having a conversation in English, it is very important to give 'feedback'. This involves using expressions that show we are listening and understand what our partner is saying. We do this by using such expressions as 'Yes,...', Mm.......', 'Well.......', 'I see what you mean.....', etc.

This is an important aspect of spoken English as a conversation could sound rather abrupt and unnatural without such expressions. In some cultures this aspect of communication is not so important, but when communicating in English, it is necessary to give feedback to your partner if you want to show you are interested and understand what has been said.

Read Conversation 1 (page 66) again and note three expressions the speakers use to give 'feedback' that indicates agreement.

1. _____

2. _____

3. _____

(Answers: page 116)

(For expressions that indicate disagreement in a polite way, see page 73.)

Non-verbal Feedback

We also use non-verbal feedback such as smiling and nodding our head (up and down) when we agree with what is being said or frowning and shaking our head (side to side) if we hear bad news, don't understand or disagree with the speaker. Someone who doesn't give feedback or show that they are listening and interested is called 'deadpan', meaning they don't show any reaction or expression on their face. So remember to give feedback!

B) Giving reasons – Justifying actions or opinions

A common word used to introduce a reason for an action or opinion in spoken English is *'because'*. eg. 'They should pay for some of the petrol *because* they often use the car.' In spoken language, we sometimes use *'seeing'* as a linking word to justify an action or opinion.

In Conversation 1, the husband suggests that the children should contribute some money towards the phone bill, then he gives a reason for (justifies) his opinion.

Read Conversation 1 and complete the following sentences from the conversation.

1) *We could ask them to chip in for the phone bill*_____

_____

Look at Conversation 1 again and find another reason why the husband thinks his kids should *chip in* for the phone bill. Use 'seeing' as a linking word to complete the following sentence.

2) *He thinks they should chip in for part of the phone bill* _____

_____

(Answer: page 116)

NOTE

We often use 'seeing' when justifying an action we have done or plan to do.

eg. 'We'll finish early today *seeing* you've all worked hard and made good progress.'

    or

 'I'm going to buy a new jacket, *seeing* I'm going for a job interview next week.'

Practice – What about you?

Think of something that you have done recently or plan to do in the future and write a sentence justifying your action using 'seeing'.

_____

_____

_____

C) Making suggestions

When discussing issues or problems and possible solutions, we often make suggestions. When making suggestions we use words such as *could, should, have to, had better* before the base verb to show attitude about 'possibility' or 'certainty'. There are examples of this in Conversation 1. Read the conversation again and complete the suggestions below.

1) Maybe we _____ **sit** down and work out a budget.

2) We will _____ **talk** to the kids about going easy on their phone calls in future.

3) Well, better still*, we _____ **ask** them to chip in for the phone bill...

Notice that the words you have written are followed by a base verb. The words you have written help to express the speaker's attitude. Some expressions show certainty; some are less certain. Which of the three expressions shows the most certainty? Check your answers on page116.

---

*Note: The expression 'Better still…' is used by speakers in informal situations when they want to respond to a suggestion by introducing a better idea than has already been suggested.

D) Agreeing and disagreeing politely

When discussing issues with family, friends or work associates, we don't always agree with each other. Therefore, it's important to express an opinion in a way that doesn't lead to an argument. The following reference list shows expressions used when agreeing, disagreeing or staying neutral in a discussion.

Expressions showing agreement	Expressions showing polite disagreement
That's for sure. Absolutely! I couldn't agree more! (means: I agree 100%) Yes, I see what you mean. That's a good point. Yes, I agree.	Yes, but I think … Yes, but on the other hand… Yes, but don't you think … You have a point but… I agree to some extent but… (means: I don't agree completely.) That may be the case, however…
Expressions indicating a neutral position	**Expressions showing stronger disagreement**
Maybe, (who knows). I can see it from both sides.	I'm sorry, I don't agree with you. I'm afraid, I must disagree with that.

When disagreeing with another person's opinion, beginning with *'Yes, but...'* demonstrates politeness by ***showing that you have listened*** to the other person's opinion before giving a different opinion.

(Units 4 - 6)

This section reviews some of the expressions which were introduced in Units 4, 5, and 6 and gives you a chance to see what you have remembered.

- Look at the pictures on the opposite page and decide what the people are saying by choosing from the expressions below.

- Match each picture with an appropriate expression by writing the correct letter in the box next to each expression.

- For extra practice, you could write the appropriate expression in the space provided in the picture.

1) Look at the price of these shoes! What a rip-off! ☐

2) My friend must've lost track of time. I'll have another coffee while I'm waiting, please. ☐

3) I feel under the weather. I'm going to lie down for a little while. ☐

4) We all chipped in to get this for you. ☐

5) Go easy on the milk or there won't be any left for me! ☐

6) You don't look well. I think you may be coming down with something. ☐

7) When did these symptoms come on? ☐

8) They look very well off, don't they? ☐

9) Sorry I can't make it. I'm pushed for time this afternoon. ☐

(Answers: page 116)

UNIT 7

TALKING ABOUT PLACES AND PREFERENCES

Before you listen to the conversation about places and preferences, look at the illustrations on the previous page. Which of the following words describe each illustration? (Answers: page 116.)

luxury	resort	remote	camping

Write your answers here: A_____ B_____

Listening for general understanding

Listen to the conversation between John and Susan and tick the correct answers.
When you have finished, you can check your answers on page 116.

1) On which day is the conversation taking place?

    a) Saturday

    b) Friday

    c) Monday

2) What is the topic of conversation?

    a) last year's trip overseas

    b) travel plans and preferred leisure activities

    c) plans to take John to the airport

3) How long is John going to take off work to travel?

    a) a week

    b) a year

    c) a month

4) During the conversation, the speakers:

    a) have different ideas about leisure activities.

    b) agree completely about leisure activities.

Now, we'll look at the everyday expressions used
in the conversation – turn to the next page.

CONVERSATION 1 - (with everyday expressions)

◂◂ Replay Conversation 1
Read the conversation as you listen to the audio recording. Do you know what the underlined words mean? They are colloquial or 'everyday' expressions.

John: I'm glad it's Friday. Bye Susan, I'll see you on Monday.

Susan: Monday? I'll see you at your **send-off** tomorrow night.

John: Send-off? I thought I was going to Peter's house for dinner... So they're having a send-off for me, are they?

Susan: Oh dear. I think I've **let the cat out of the bag**. But nobody told me to keep it **hush hush**.

John: Don't worry. I won't tell anyone you **spilled the beans**. It'll be fun!

Susan: Oh good ... I hear that you're taking a year off work to travel. Where're you planning to go?

John: Well, I want to see as much of the world as possible but I want to get **off the beaten track** and away from **the rat race** of city life.

Susan: Well, it sounds like you'll be **on the go**.

John: I sure will and I'll have to **rough it** but I love camping so I'll be **in my element**!

Susan: Really?... Well, that's not my idea of a fun time. I'd prefer to **live it up** at a resort where I'd **be waited on hand and foot**. Somewhere I could **let my hair down**, party at night and then **take it easy** beside the pool during the day.

John: Oh no. It'd **drive me up the wall** to lie around a pool all day. That's **not my cup of tea** at all.

Susan: Oh well, **to each his own**. I'll see you on Saturday anyway. Oh, and please don't tell anyone I **let the cat out of the bag**.

John: Don't worry, I won't. I'll definitely **keep it under wraps**.

Now let's see what the underlined expressions mean - look at the next page.

CONVERSATION 2 - (explanation of everyday expressions)

***Compare Conversation 1 with Conversation 2** - You will see that some of the words are different but the meaning is the same in both conversations. Find the underlined expressions in Conversation 1, then underline the words with the same meaning in Conversation 2. For example: <u>send-off</u> (Conversation 1) = <u>farewell party</u> (Conversation 2)*

John: I'm glad it's Friday. Bye Susan, I'll see you on Monday.

Susan: Monday? I'll see you at your <u>farewell party</u> tomorrow night.

John: Farewell party? I thought I was going to Peter's house for dinner....So they're having a farewell party for me, are they?

Susan: Oh dear. I think I've revealed a secret. But nobody told me to keep it secret.

John: Don't worry. I won't tell anyone that you revealed the secret. It'll be fun!

Susan: Oh good... I hear that you're taking a year off from work to travel. Where're you planning to go?

John: Well, I want to see as much of the world as possible but I want to get away from the populated areas and away from the constantly busy competition of city life.

Susan: Well it sounds like you'll be busy.

John: I sure will and I'll have to live without basic comforts but I love camping so I'll be in my preferred situation!

Susan: Really?... Well, that's not my idea of a fun time. I'd prefer to live in luxury at a resort where I'd have all my needs attended to. Somewhere that I could behave very informally, party at night and then relax beside the pool during the day.

John: Oh no…It would greatly irritate me to lie around a pool all day. That's not something that interests me at all.

Susan: Oh well, everyone has his/her own preference. I'll see you on Saturday anyway. Oh, and please don't tell anyone that I revealed the secret.

John: Don't worry. I won't. I will definitely keep the information a secret.

Important note:
The language used in Conversation 2 (above) may seem easier to understand when compared with Conversation 1. However, the 'everyday' expressions used in Conversation 1 are used extensively by speakers of English. Therefore it is important to become familiar with the everyday expressions used by the speakers in **Conversation 1**.

◀◀ **Replay Conversation 1**

Listen to the conversation again and fill in the missing words. You may have to listen more than once. Don't worry about your spelling as this exercise focuses on listening skills. You can check your spelling later.

John: I'm glad it's Friday. Bye Susan, I'll see you on Monday.

Susan: Monday? I'll see you at your **send-_____** tomorrow night.

John: Send-off? I thought I was going to Peter's house for dinner..... So they're having a send-off for me, are they?

Susan: Oh dear. I think I've **let the cat out of the _____**. But nobody told me to keep it _____ **hush**.

John: Don't worry. I won't tell anyone you **spilled the _____**. It'll be fun!

Susan: Oh good ...I hear that you're taking a year off work to travel. Where're you planning to go?

John: Well, I want to see as much of the world as possible but I want to get **_____ the beaten track** and away from **the _____ race** of city life.

Susan: Well, it sounds like you'll be **on the _____**.

John: I sure will and I'll have to **_____ it** but I love camping so I'll be **in my _____**!

Susan: Really?...Well, that's not my idea of a fun time. I'd prefer to **live it _____** at a resort where I'd **be waited on _____ and foot**. Somewhere I could **let my _____ down**, party at night and then **take it _____** beside the pool during the day.

John: Oh no. It'd **drive me up the _____** to lie around a pool all day. That's **not my _____ of tea** at all.

Susan: Oh well, **to each his own**. I'll see you on Saturday anyway. Oh, and please don't tell anyone I **let the _____ out of the bag**.

John: Don't worry, I won't. I'll definitely **keep it _____ wraps**.

Now check your answers by checking this page with
CONVERSATION 1.

In order to become more familiar with these new everyday expressions:

◄◄ **Replay Conversation 1**
1) **Listen and tick the boxes** ☑ **next to the expressions as you hear them.**
2) **Write in the definitions you can remember. (One has been done as an example.)**
   Check your answers with the reference list on page 128.

☐	a send-off...................….……	_a farewell party_
☐	let the cat out of the bag.............…	
☐	hush hush...............................……	
☐	spill the beans...............................	
☐	off the beaten track......................	
☐	the rat race...............................	
☐	on the go.................................	
☐	to rough it.................................	
☐	in (my) element......................……	
☐	live it up..................................	
☐	be waited on hand and foot..........	
☐	let (my) hair down.......................	
☐	take it easy.................................	
☐	drive (me) up the wall..................	
☐	**not** my cup of tea.....................…	
☐	to each his own...........................	
☐	keep (it) under wraps.............…..	

LANGUAGE NOTES:

*The expression '**not** _my cup of tea_' is usually used in the negative to refer to an
    activity or thing that is **not** liked by the speaker.

CROSSWORD – VOCABULARY REVISION

Complete the sentences, using the everyday expressions which have been listed below. You can use the clues in brackets ( ) at the end of each sentence to help you. Then complete the crossword using the everyday expressions you have written. The first one has been done as an example.

rat race	rough it	spill the beans	take it easy	~~let the cat out of the bag~~
under wraps	on the go	waited on hand and foot	live it up	up the wall

ACROSS

1) I'm sorry I **_let the cat out of the bag_** about your wedding plans. (revealed a secret)

3) I've been ___ _____ ____ all day, preparing for the party tonight. (busy)

5) I'm very angry with Tom because I asked him not to _____ ____ _____ to everyone about our plans. (reveal the secret)

7) We had a wonderful holiday. We were _____ ___ _____ ____ _____ all week. (had all our needs attended to)

9) Don't worry, I'll keep your plan _____ _____. (as a secret)

DOWN

2) I'm going to _____ ___ _____ on the weekend. I've had a very busy week. (relax)

4) When we were first married, we had to _____ ___ because we didn't have enough money to buy any furniture. (live without basic comforts)

6) I am planning to move to the country to get away from the _____ _____. (constantly busy competition of city life)

8) The people next door drive me ___ ____ _____. They play loud music all day. (irritate me)

10) I'm going to _____ ___ ___ when I go to an expensive resort next month! (live in luxury)

(Answers: page 116)

FOCUS ON SPOKEN LANGUAGE

A) Using intonation to check meaning

As you have learnt in previous units, when speaking in English, we often use 'intonation', or the rise and fall of our voice, to express meaning. For example, when we are confused, surprised or think we have misunderstood something that has been said, we may repeat the word or expression with a rise and fall tone to show we don't understand or need the information repeated.

◀◀ Replay Conversation 1
Listen to the first part of *Conversation 1* on the audio recording again as you read the conversation below. You will notice two examples where the speakers have used this conversation strategy (as shown by the arrows ⤴◣).

John: I'm glad it's Friday. Bye Susan, I'll see you on Monday.

Susan: *Monday?* I'll see you at your send-off tomorrow night.

John: *Send-off?* I thought I was going to Peter's house for dinner... So they're having a send-

off for me, are they?

Did you hear the rising and falling intonation pattern? Practise the sentences above using rising and falling intonation for the underlined words.

CONVERSATION FILLERS

In spoken English, speakers often begin a reply or comment with a word such as *'Well'* or *'Oh'*. As we saw in Unit 6, one reason for this is to give feedback and show we are listening. Read Conversation 1 of this Unit again and notice how many times these expressions are used.

Using expressions such as *'Well'* or *'Oh, well'* at the beginning of a reply also gives speakers more time to think about their reply if they don't agree with what has been said.
For example, Susan's reply at the end of the conversation: *'Oh well,* to each his own':
'Oh well...' makes the comment less abrupt and more conversational.

B) Talking about preferences

The word 'would' is a modal auxiliary verb. This means it is used along with a main verb to express attitude or degrees of certainty. Speakers use 'would' to talk about possible future situations and to express preferences.

Find and underline the modal auxiliary verb 'would' or its contracted form, 'd, in the conversation below. Note that in conversational English, 'would' is generally contracted to 'd.

John: I want to see as much of the world as possible but I want to get off the beaten track and away from the rat race of city life.

Susan: Well, it sounds like you'll be on the go.

John: I sure will and I'll have to rough it but I love camping so I'll be in my element!

Susan: Really?..... Well, that's not my idea of a fun time. I'd prefer to live it up at a resort where I'd be waited on hand and foot. Somewhere I could let my hair down, party at night and then take it easy beside the pool during the day.

John: Oh no. It'd drive me up the wall to lie around a pool all day. That's not my cup of tea at all.

Susan: Oh well, to each his own. I'll see you on Saturday anyway. Oh, and please don't tell anyone I let the cat out of the bag.

John: Don't worry, I won't. I'll definitely keep it under wraps.

Note that in the conversation above, when the speakers use 'would', they are not talking about definite situations but are talking about their 'ideas' or 'preferences' regarding travel and leisure activities.

Ways of expressing preference:

Look at the following ways of expressing preference.

1) I'*d prefer to live it up* at a resort.

2) I'*d rather live it up* at a resort.

3) I'*d sooner live it up* at a resort.

The meaning in each of the above sentences is the same but the grammatical structure is a little different. Can you see how the first sentence is different to the other two?

Check your answer on page 117.

WHAT ABOUT YOU?

What kind of leisure activities do you prefer? Are you 'in your element' when camping like John or do you prefer to 'live it up' at a resort like Susan?

Choose from the expressions below to explain your preference.

For example: *I'd prefer to:*

get off the beaten track.

get away from the rat race.

live it up at a resort.

be waited on hand and foot.

take it easy beside a pool.

let my hair down.

Write about your preference for leisure activities.

_____

_____

_____

_____

C) Ellipsis – leaving words out in short replies

In Unit 5, you saw that in conversational speech, speakers do not always use complete sentences if the meaning is clear to both speakers without using a complete sentence. Look at the short replies taken from Conversation 1. Finish the incomplete, short replies to make the intended meaning clear.

Susan: Well, it sounds like you'll be on the go.

John: *I sure will* _____ and I'll have to rough it…

Susan: …please don't tell anyone I let the cat out of the bag.

John: *Don't worry, I won't* _____

I'll definitely keep it under wraps.

Answers, page 117.

UNIT 8

MAKING AN ARRANGEMENT BY TELEPHONE

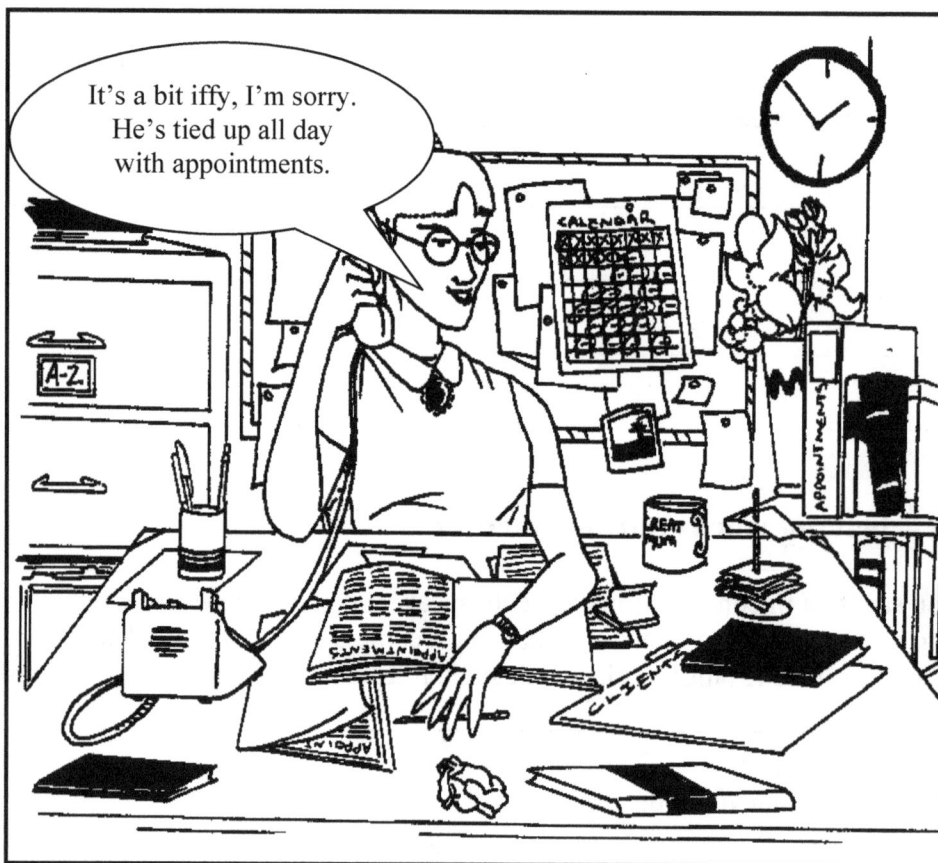

At some time you will probably need to make an arrangement by telephone. This unit provides some useful information about the conventions of making an arrangement by phone, as well as presenting some everyday expressions you may hear when making an arrangement by telephone.

Listening for general understanding

Listen to this conversation in which someone is trying to make an arrangement for a trades person to do some household repairs. The customer is speaking to a receptionist. (Unit 8 on the audio recording.) As you listen, tick the correct answers below.

When you have finished you can check you answers on page 117.

_____

1) The customer is phoning:

        a) a carpenter

        b) a plumber

        c) an electrician

2) What time can the trades person visit?

        a) 9 o'clock

        b) 5 o'clock

        c) 6 o'clock

3) What is the customer's name?

        a) Mr Ford

        b) Mr Ward

        c) Mr Sword

Now, we'll look at the everyday expressions used in the conversation – turn to the next page.

CONVERSATION 1 (with everyday expressions)

◄◄ Replay Conversation 1
Read this conversation as you listen to the audio recording. Do you know what the _underlined_ words mean? They are colloquial or everyday expressions.

Receptionist: Good afternoon, Davison's Plumbing. **Hold the line** please.............

Sorry to keep you waiting. Can I help you?

Customer: Yes. Is that Davison's Plumbing?

Receptionist: Yes, it is.

Customer: I'd like a plumber to **take a look at** my toilet please. It seems to be blocked.

Receptionist: Certainly. We're a bit **snowed under** this afternoon so the plumber

may not be able to **make it** there until tomorrow. Is that OK?

Customer: Not really. We're **in a fix** because we've only got one toilet.

Is it possible for him to come sooner?

Receptionist: Mm. It's a bit **iffy**, I'm sorry. He's completely **tied up** with appointments all day... but

look, if you'd like to **hang on** a minute, I'll try to **get in touch** with him

and see how he's **fixed for time**.

Customer: OK. Thank you…

Receptionist: … Hello…Well you're in luck. He's had **a good run** with his work today

and his last appointment was **called off**, so he can **fit you in** at about 5 o'clock.

Customer: Oh great! Could you give me **a rough idea** of the cost?

Receptionist: No sorry, not until he **sorts out** the cause of the problem, but don't worry

he'll **fill you in** on the cost before he **goes ahead with** the work.

Customer: OK. Thanks very much for your help.

Receptionist: You're welcome. Could I have your name and address please?

Customer: Yes, it's Mr. Ford.

Receptionist: Sorry, I didn't **catch** that. Did you say Sword?

Customer: No. Ford. F for father, - O - R - D. My address is.................

Now let's see what the underlined expressions mean - look at the next page.

CONVERSATION 2 (explanation of everyday expressions)

Compare Conversation 1 with Conversation 2 - You will see that some of the words are different but the meaning is the same in both conversations. Find the underlined expressions in Conversation 1, then underline the words with the same meaning in Conversation 2. For example: *Hold the line* (Conversation 1) = *Wait a moment* (Conversation 2)

Receptionist:	Good afternoon, Davison's Plumbing. <u>Wait a moment</u> please............. Sorry to keep you waiting. Can I help you?
Customer:	Yes. Is that Davison's Plumbing?
Receptionist:	Yes, it is.
Customer:	I'd like a plumber to inspect my toilet please. It seems to be blocked.
Receptionist:	Certainly. We're a bit busy with work this afternoon so the plumber may not be able to arrive there until tomorrow. Is that OK?
Customer:	Not really. We're in a difficult situation because we've only got one toilet. Is it possible for him to come sooner?
Receptionist:	Mm. It's a bit uncertain, I'm sorry. He's completely involved with appointments all day… but look, if you'd like to wait a minute, I'll try to contact/speak to him and see how much (spare) time he has available.
Customer:	OK. Thank you…
Receptionist:	… Hello …Well you're in luck. He's made good progress with his work today and his last appointment was cancelled, so he can make time available for you at about 5 o'clock.
Customer:	Oh great! Could you give me an approximate idea of the cost?
Receptionist:	No sorry, not until he determines/finds the cause of the problem, but don't worry he'll give you information on the cost before he starts the work.
Customer:	OK. Thanks very much for your help.
Receptionist:	You're welcome. Could I have your name and address please?
Customer:	Yes, it's Mr. Ford.
Receptionist:	Sorry, I didn't hear/understand that. Did you say Sword?
Customer:	No. Ford. F for father, - O - R - D. My address is…

Important note:
The language used in Conversation 2 (above) may seem easier to understand when compared with Conversation 1. However, the 'everyday' expressions used in Conversation 1 are used extensively by speakers of English. Therefore it is important to become familiar with the everyday expressions used by the speakers in **Conversation 1**.

◀◀ **Replay Conversation 1**
Listen to the conversation again and fill in the missing words. You may have to listen more than once. (Don't worry about your spelling as this exercise focuses on listening skills - you can check your spelling later.)

Receptionist: Good afternoon, Davison's Plumbing. ***Hold the*** _____ please.............
Sorry to keep you waiting. Can I help you?

Customer: Yes. Is that Davison's Plumbing?

Receptionist: Yes, it is.

Customer: I'd like a plumber to _____ ***a*** _____ ***at*** my toilet please. It seems to be blocked.

Receptionist: Certainly. We're a bit _____ ***under*** this afternoon so the plumber may not be able to _____ ***it*** there until tomorrow. Is that OK?

Customer: Not really. We're ***in a*** _____ because we've only got one toilet.
Is it possible for him to come sooner?

Receptionist: Mm. It's a bit _____, I'm sorry. He's completely ***tied up*** with appointments all day … but look, if you'd like to ***hang on*** a minute, I'll try to ***get in touch*** with him and see how he's _____ ***for time***.

Customer: OK. Thank you…

Receptionist: ... Hello… Well you're in luck. He's had ***a good*** _____ with his work today and his last appointment was ***called*** _____, so he can ***fit you*** _____ at about 5 o'clock.

Customer: Oh great! Could you give me ***a*** _____ ***idea*** of the cost?

Receptionist: No sorry, not until he ***sorts*** _____ the cause of the problem, but don't worry he'll ***fill you*** _____ on the cost before he ***goes*** _____ ***with*** the work.

Customer: OK. Thanks very much for your help.

Receptionist: You're welcome. Could I have your name and address please?

Customer: Yes, it's Mr. Ford.

Receptionist: Sorry, I didn't _____ that. Did you say Sword?

Customer: No. Ford. F for father, - O - R - D. My address is.................

Now check your answers by checking this page with
CONVERSATION 1.

In order to become more familiar with these new everyday expressions:

◀◀ **Replay Conversation 1**
1) **Listen and tick the boxes ✓ next to the expressions as you hear them.**
2) **Write in the definitions you can remember. (One has been done as an example.)**
   Check your answers with the reference list on page 129.

☐ Hold the line...................……	*Wait a moment* _____
☐ take a look at……………...……	_____
☐ snowed under................................	_____
☐ to make it................................	_____
☐ in a fix................................	_____
☐ iffy................................	_____
☐ tied up………...............…………	_____
☐ hang on................................	_____
☐ get in touch................................	_____
☐ see how (he's) fixed for time……..	_____
☐ a good run................................	_____
☐ called off…………………………	_____
☐ *fit (you) in................................	_____
☐ a rough idea	_____
☐ sort out................................	_____
☐ *fill (you) in................................	_____
☐ goes ahead with ....……	_____
☐ catch................................……	_____

---

*LANGUAGE NOTE:

Note the difference in meaning between the phrasal verbs 'fit in' and 'fill in' in the following sentences:
'The doctor will *fit you in* on Monday.' (make time for you)
'The doctor will *fill you in* on Monday.' (give you information/details)

See Unit 9, Part 6D for information on the position of pronouns in some phrasal verbs.

CROSSWORD – VOCABULARY REVISION

Complete the sentences, using the everyday expressions which have been listed below. You can use the clues in brackets ( ) at the end of each sentence to help you. Then complete the crossword using the everyday expressions you have written. The first one has been done as an example.

called off	a rough idea	~~hold the line~~	make it	a good run	iffy
catch	sort out	a fix	snowed under	take a look	get in touch

ACROSS

1) Could you ***hold the line*** please while I connect you to Mr Smith's extension number. (wait while speaking on the telephone)

3) The business meeting has been _____ ___ . (cancelled)

5) We've had __ _____ ____ with this project. We'll be finished soon. (made good progress)

7) Don't worry. We can _____ ____ this problem. (find the answer to)

9) Could you _____ __ _____ at my car please? It's making a strange noise. (inspect)

11) Do you have __ _____ _____ how long it will take to do the job? (an approximate idea)

DOWN

2) I'll be home late tonight because we're _____ _____ at the office. (very busy)

4) We'll _____ ___ _____ when your order is ready. (contact you)

6) It's ____ whether the cricket will continue due to the heavy rain. (uncertain)

8) I won't be able to _____ ___ until 9 o' clock as the trains are late. (arrive)

10) Did you _____ what he just said? I couldn't hear him. (hear/understand)

12) I'm in __ _____ because I don't have any money to pay my expenses. (a difficult situation)

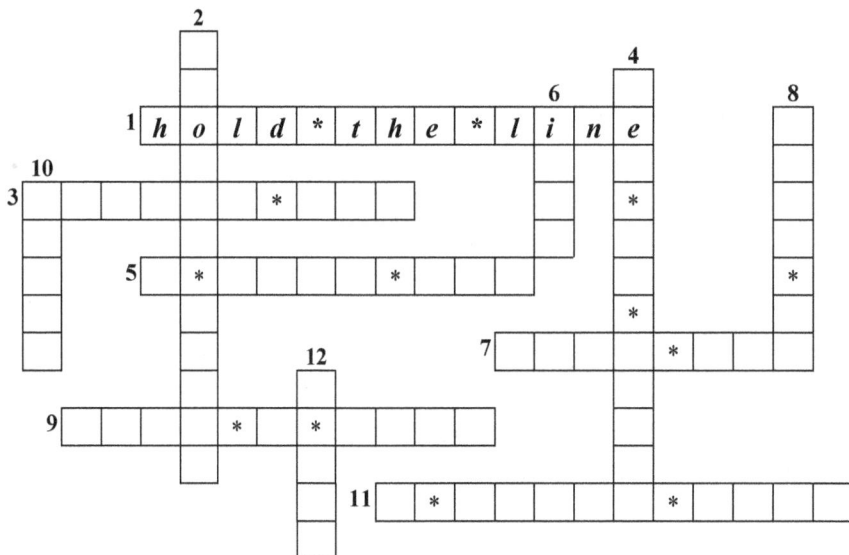

Check your answers on page 117.

FOCUS ON SPOKEN LANGUAGE

A) Stages in a phone request for service

A telephone request for service generally has the following stages:

1) Greeting and identification
2) Reason for the call
3) Making enquiries/arrangements (time and cost)
4) Giving and checking name and address
5) Closing the conversation

Find each of the stages in the following conversation and draw a line between each stage.
The first one has been done for you. (Answers: page 118)

Receptionist:	Good afternoon, Davison's Plumbing. Hold the line please............. Sorry to keep you waiting. Can I help you? **1**
Customer:	Yes. Is that Davison's Plumbing?
Receptionist:	Yes, it is.
Customer:	I'd like a plumber to take a look at my toilet please. It seems to be blocked.
Receptionist:	Certainly. We're a bit snowed under this afternoon so the plumber may not be able to make it there until tomorrow. Is that OK?
Customer:	Not really. We're in a fix because we've only got one toilet. Is it possible for him to come sooner?
Receptionist:	Mm. It's a bit iffy, I'm sorry. He's completely tied up with appointments all day…but look, if you'd like to hang on a minute, I'll try to get in touch with him and see how he's fixed for time.
Customer:	OK. Thank you.
Receptionist:	Hello ... Well you're in luck. He's had a good run with his work today and his last appointment was called off, so he can fit you in at about 5 o'clock.
Customer:	Oh great! Could you give me a rough idea of the cost?
Receptionist:	No sorry, not until he sorts out the cause of the problem but don't worry he'll fill you in on the cost before he goes ahead with the work.
Customer:	OK. Thanks very much for your help.
Receptionist:	You're welcome. Could I have your name and address please?
Customer:	Yes, it's Mr Ford.
Receptionist:	Sorry, I didn't catch that. Did you say Sword?
Customer:	No. Ford. F for father,-O-R-D. My address is number 12 Mar Street, Newtown.
Receptionist:	Could you spell the name of your suburb please.
Customer:	Yes it's N-E-W-T-O-W-N.
Receptionist:	OK thanks. We'll see you this afternoon, at about 5 o' clock.
Customer:	OK thanks. Bye.
Receptionist:	Bye.

Giving your name and address on the telephone

- Notice that in the above conversation, it was necessary for the customer to *spell* his surname and suburb.

Remember! If you need to arrange for someone to come to your home, it's important to be able to spell your surname, street name and suburb aloud.

B) Checking information given on the telephone

◀◀ Replay Conversation 1

Listen to the first part of Conversation 1 again and notice how quickly the receptionist says the company name. It is often difficult to hear a name clearly on the telephone when it is spoken quickly, especially if English is not your first language.

How can a caller overcome this problem? Read the first few lines of Conversation 1 and check the words the customer uses to make sure he has contacted the correct company.
Complete the customer's part of the conversation below.

Receptionist: Good afternoon, Davison's Plumbing. Hold the line please...

Sorry to keep you waiting. Can I help you?

Customer: Yes. _____

Receptionist: Yes, it is.

Check your answers on page 118.

C) Using polite language when requesting service

When dealing with service people such as tradespeople, shop assistants, or receptionists it's important to use polite language when we are asking for something. For example, in Conversation 1 the customer uses expressions such as:

'*Is it possible* for him to come sooner?' and '*Could you* give me a rough idea of the cost?'

When requesting service it would sound very rude if we spoke too directly by saying:
'*Tell him to come sooner*' or '*Give me some idea of the cost*', as these sentences sound like commands.

Look at the following sentences and change them to a more polite form using,
'*Could I..........................please.*'   or   '*Could you..............................please.*'

The first one has been done as an example.

1) Pass me a bag.   *Could you pass me a bag, please?*

2) Give the manager this message. _____

3) Show me the blue shirt there. _____

4) Give me a bottle of Coke.   _____

Check your answers on page 118.

D) Pronunciation of words ending with 'ed'

The pronunciation of 'ed' endings of past tense verbs can be confusing for learners. In some words, the 'ed' is pronounced as an extra syllable but in other words, the 'ed' is pronounced as part of the preceding syllable. The following exercise and explanation will provide some guidelines.

- Read the extract from Conversation 1 below and <u>underline</u> five words with 'ed' endings.
- Now listen to the conversation. Are the underlined words pronounced as one or two syllables?

Customer: I'd like a plumber to take a look at my toilet please. It seems to be blocked.
Receptionist: Certainly. We're a bit snowed under this afternoon so the plumber
               may not be able to make it there until tomorrow. Is that OK?
Customer: Not really. We're in a fix because we've only got one toilet.
               Is it possible for him to come sooner?
Receptionist: Mm. It's a bit iffy, I'm sorry. He's completely tied up with appointments all day... but
               look, if you'd like to hang on a minute, I'll try to get in touch with him
               and see how he's fixed for time.
Customer: OK. Thank you...
Receptionist: ... Hello...Well you're in luck. He's had a good run with his work today
               and his last appointment was called off, so he can fit you in at about 5 o'clock.

Answers: page 119.

Read the following general rules about 'ed' endings

The pronunciation of 'ed' at the end of a word depends on the sound that comes directly before it.

- 'ed' is pronounced as an extra syllable only when added to words which end in the sounds 'd' or 't'. In these words, the 'ed' endings on words are pronounced as an extra syllable.
  For example: the word 'en<u>d</u>ed' has two syllables 'end-ed'
               the word 'pa<u>tt</u>ed' has two syllables 'patt-ed'

- However, in most words, an 'ed' ending becomes part of the preceding syllable, to form a one-syllable word. For example: the word 'missed' is pronounced as one syllable /mɪst/;
               the word 'billed' is pronounced as one syllable /bɪld/.

Practice
Using the above 'rules', write the following words in the correct column below.

needed	worked	started	looked	washed	phoned
'ed' pronounced as an extra syllable			**'ed' pronounced as part of the preceding syllable**		

You can check your answers on page 119.

UNIT 9

AT A SOCIAL GATHERING

Social gatherings provide an opportunity for friends to meet informally, as well as an opportunity for people to make new friends. What kinds of things do people talk about when they meet for the first time at a party (or any social occasion)?

Listening for general understanding

Listen to the conversation between Len (a guest) and Bill (one of the hosts), who are meeting for the first time at a barbecue organised by Bill and Kate (Unit 9 on the audio recording). The conversation contains 'everyday expressions' that will be explained later in the unit - so don't worry if you don't understand every word. This time you are only listening for general understanding of the conversation. As you listen, tick the correct answers below. (There may be more than one correct answer.)

When you have finished you can check your answers on page 119.

1) Bill introduces himself as:

    a) Kate's brother

    b) Kate's husband

2) Len knows Kate because:

    a) they play the same sport

    b) they are work colleagues
       (they work for the same company)

3) Which topics do the men talk about:

    a) the weather

    b) politics

    c) a person they both know

    d) their work

    e) sport/hobbies

    f) religion

    g) local area/home

Now, we'll look at the everyday expressions used in the conversation – turn to the next page.

CONVERSATION 1 (with everyday expressions)

◀◀ Replay Conversation 1
Read this conversation as you listen to the audio recording. Do you know what the underlined words mean? They are colloquial or 'everyday' expressions.

Bill: Hello. You must be Len. I'm Bill, Kate's husband.

Len: Oh, hello Bill. Nice to meet you. Thanks for inviting me.

Bill: You're welcome. Kate and I thought it was **about time** we had **a get together** and met each other's work colleagues. Kate tells me you've just joined the company.

Len: Yes. I've been there about four months now. Kate's been very helpful, **showing me the ropes**.

Bill: Yes, she enjoys her job.

Len: What line of work are you in Bill?

Bill: I'm a builder. I work with Joe and Kevin over there.

Len: Oh yes, I met Kevin earlier. Well, it's a **top spot** you have here Bill.

Bill: Thanks. Yes, it **has a lot going for it**. It **beats** living in the city.

Len: **You can say that again**. Have you lived here long?

Bill: Oh...**going on** three years now. **Mind you** the house wasn't like this when we moved in. It's taken **the good part of** three years to **do it up**. But I enjoy decorating. It's a hobby really.

Len: Well, it's **a credit to you**. It looks **great**.

Bill: Thanks very much. Can I get you another drink?

Len: No thanks, I'm OK. I'm playing golf first thing in the morning, so I want to **have my wits about me**.

Bill: Oh, Kate and I play golf **now and again**. We should get together for a game sometime.

Len: OK, that sounds good, **I'll take you up on that**. By the way, have you been following the tennis? Who won last night?

Bill: I'm sorry, I don't know. I'm not really **up on** tennis. I watch a game on TV **once in a while** but I'm not really **into** it. Come on, I'll introduce you to Joe - he'll be **up on** the latest results.

Now let's see what the underlined expressions mean - look at the next page.

CONVERSATION 2 - (explanation of everyday expressions)

Compare Conversation 1 with Conversation 2 - You will see that some of the words are different but the meaning is the same in both conversations. Find the underlined expressions in Conversation 1, then underline the words with the same meaning in Conversation 2. For example: *about time* (Conversation 1) = *timely* (Conversation 2)

Bill: Hello. You must be Len. I'm Bill, Kate's husband.

Len: Oh, hello Bill. Nice to meet you. Thanks for inviting me.

Bill: You're welcome. Kate and I thought it was <u>timely (we should have done it before now)</u> we had a social gathering and met each other's work colleagues. Kate tells me you've just joined the company.

Len: Yes. I've been there about four months now. Kate's been very helpful, explaining how to do things.

Bill: Yes, she enjoys her job.

Len: What line of work are you in Bill?

Bill: I'm a builder. I work with Joe and Kevin over there.

Len: Oh yes, I met Kevin earlier. Well, it's a nice place you have here Bill.

Bill: Thanks. Yes, it has a lot of advantages. It is better than living in the city.

Len: I agree with you. Have you lived here long?

Bill: Oh... almost three years now. However, the house wasn't like this when we moved in. It's taken almost three years to repair/improve it. But I enjoy decorating. It's a hobby really.

Len: Well, it's something you should be very proud of. It looks very good/excellent.

Bill: Thanks very much. Can I get you another drink?

Len: No thanks, I'm OK. I'm playing golf first thing in the morning, so I want to be alert/clear in my head.

Bill: Oh, Kate and I play golf sometimes. We should get together for a game sometime.

Len: OK, that sounds good, I'll accept that offer. By the way, have you been following the tennis? Who won last night?

Bill: I'm sorry, I don't know. I'm not really knowledgeable about tennis. I watch a game on TV occasionally but I'm not really involved/interested in it. Come on, I'll introduce you to Joe - he'll be knowledgeable about the latest results.

Important note:
The language used in Conversation 2 (above) may seem easier to understand when compared with Conversation 1. However, the 'everyday' expressions used in Conversation 1 are used extensively by speakers of English. Therefore it is important to become familiar with the everyday expressions used by the speakers in **Conversation 1**.

◀◀ **Replay Conversation 1**
Listen to the conversation again and fill in the missing words. You may have to listen more than once. Don't worry about your spelling as this exercise focuses on listening skills. You can check your spelling later.

Bill: Hello. You must be Len. I'm Bill, Kate's husband.

Len: Oh, hello Bill. Nice to meet you. Thanks for inviting me.

Bill: You're welcome. Kate and I thought it was **about time** we had **a_____ together** and met each other's work colleagues. Kate tells me you've just joined the company.

Len: Yes. I've been there about four months now. Kate's been very helpful, **showing me the**
_____.

Bill: Yes, she enjoys her job.

Len: What line of work are you in Bill?

Bill: I'm a builder. I work with Joe and Kevin over there.

Len: Oh yes, I met Kevin earlier. Well, it's a _____ **spot** you have here Bill.

Bill: Thanks. Yes, it **has a lot** _____ **for it**. It **beats** living in the city.

Len: **You can say that** _____. Have you lived here long?

Bill: Oh....**going on** three years now. _____ **you** the house wasn't like this when we moved in. It's taken **the** _____ **part of** three years to **do it** _____. But I enjoy decorating. It's a hobby really.

Len: Well, it's **a** _____ **to you**. It looks **great**.

Bill: Thanks very much. Can I get you another drink?

Len: No thanks, I'm OK. I'm playing golf first thing in the morning, so I want to **have my**
_____ **about me**.

Bill: Oh, Kate and I play golf **now and** _____. We should get together for a game sometime.

Len: OK, that sounds good, **I'll** _____ **you up on that**. By the way, have you been following the tennis? Who won last night?

Bill: I'm sorry, I don't know. I'm not really _____ **on** tennis. I watch a game on TV
_____ **in a while** but I'm not really ____ it. Come on, I'll introduce you to Joe - he'll be up on the latest results.

Check you answers by comparing this page with CONVERSATION 1, page 98.

In order to become more familiar with these new everyday expressions:

◀◀ **Replay Conversation 1**
1) **Listen and tick the boxes ☑ next to the expressions as you hear them.**
2) **Write the definitions you can remember (One has been done as an example.)**
   Check your answers with the reference list on page 130.

☐ about time …………………..……….. *timely (but it should have happened before now)*

☐ a get together……………………......……

☐ showing (me) the ropes ……………......…

☐ a top spot………………….………..

☐ (has) a lot going for it………………..………

☐ beats……….……………………………

☐ You can say that again…………………

☐ going on ………………………………

☐ mind you……………..…………………..

☐ the good part of ……………………..………

☐ do (it) up …………………………………

☐ It's a credit to you………………………

☐ great………………………………………..

☐ have my wits about me……………..……

☐ now and again…………………………......

☐ I'll take you up on that………………..

☐ up on (something) ………………………

☐ once in a while………………………..

☐ into……………………………………..

LANGUAGE NOTES:

When we use the expression, *'about time'* to describe the timing of an event, we often mean that it should have happened earlier; it is overdue. For example:
'It's about time the train arrived' means *'The train should have arrived before now'*.
'It's about time I cleaned my room.' means *'I should have cleaned my room before now.'*

In Conversation 1, Len asked Bill, '…have you been following *the* tennis?' The definite article 'the' was used here as both speakers understood that Len was referring specifically to the tennis competition currently in the news.

CROSSWORD – VOCABULARY REVISION

Complete the sentences, using the everyday expressions which have been listed below. You can use the clues in brackets ( ) at the end of each sentence to help you. Then complete the crossword using the everyday expressions you have written. The first one has been done as an example.

a get together	up on	~~now and again~~	mind you	into	a credit to you
beats	take you up on	do up	good part of	about time

ACROSS

1) Since we've all grown up, I only see my cousins **_now and again_**. (sometimes/occasionally)

3) In my opinion, travelling by train _____ travelling by bus. (is better than)

5) Are you ___ ___ the latest desktop publishing software? I need some help. (knowledgeable about)

7) I've been working as a chef for the _____ _____ ___ six years. (almost)

9) I'll _____ _____ ___ ___ your offer to help me paint the house. (accept the offer)

11) We're going to borrow some money to ___ ___ the house before we sell it. (repair/improve)

DOWN

2) He's always late. _____ _____, he has a long way to travel. (but/however)

4) John's having __ _____ _____ at his house tonight. Are you going? (social gathering)

6) Your garden is __ _____ ____ _____. It's so beautiful. (something to be proud of)

8) It's _____ _____ you arrived! I've been waiting ages. (you should have arrived before now)

10) He's really _____ fishing but I don't like it. (interested/involved in)

(Answers: page 119)

FOCUS ON SPOKEN LANGUAGE

A) Making 'Small Talk' – appropriate topics

When we meet someone for the first time socially, we have to think of things to talk about to be friendly and get to know the person. This is referred to as *'making small talk'* and means talking about general, rather than personal topics.

People of different cultures have different ideas about what are appropriate and inappropriate topics of conversation when speaking with someone they don't know well.

Which of the topics in the box below do people of *your culture* consider appropriate subjects to discuss when meeting someone for the first time?

Do you think your answer to the above question would be the same in all cultures?

the weather	political issues	family	the surrounding area
sport	work/profession	religion	sexual issues

Now look at the following questions. Which do you think would be *inappropriate* (not suitable) questions to ask someone you have just met at a party or social gathering?
Put a cross (X) next to inappropriate questions. Then check the comments on page 120.

TOPIC

JOB

FAMILY

HOME

QUESTIONS

☐ What type of work do you do?
☐ How much do you earn?

☐ Is your family here with you?
☐ Are you married?
☐ Why aren't you married?
☐ Do you have children?
☐ Why don't you have any children?

☐ Do you live near here?
☐ How much did your house cost?
☐ What is your address?

B) Starting a conversation and keeping it going

If you don't know the other people at a social gathering or you don't feel confident because your language background is different to most people at the party, it is not always easy to start a conversation. However, there are strategies that will help you to start a conversation and keep it going.

Look at the following examples of informal introductions:

'Hello. I'm Bill.' (Note: People generally introduce themselves by their first name in informal situations.)

'Hello. I don't think we've met. I'm Bill.'

'Hi there. We haven't met, have we? I'm Bill.'

'Hello. You must be Len, I'm Bill.'

(Note: The phrase, 'You must be…' is used when the speaker is quite sure who they are speaking to.)

Read Conversation 1 again (page 98). Write Bill's introduction on the line provided below.

Bill: _____

You will notice that when Bill introduced himself, he gave additional information about himself that would help the conversation to continue. He introduced himself as 'Kate's husband' because he knew that Len worked with Kate. In other words, both speakers knew 'Kate', so they had a 'common topic' to begin their conversation.

One way of starting a conversation at a social gathering is by asking, 'How do you know …(the host of the social gathering)?' This may give you a 'common topic' to begin your conversation. Once you begin the conversation, it will then be easier to continue to talk about other topics.

Practice

◄◄ Replay Conversation 1

Listen to Conversation 1 again, and notice the order in which Len and Bill talked about different topics. Number the boxes in the order in which the topics were discussed. The first topic has been numbered.

☐ someone they both know   ☐ work/jobs   ☐ their hobbies

1 their names (who they are)   ☐ home/nearby area   ☐ sport in the news

(You can check your answers on page 120.)

C) Revision - Using 'question tags' to begin a conversation

In unit 2, you learned how question tags are used in conversational speech. Finish the following 'conversation starters' with the correct 'question tag'. After you have checked your answers on page 120, add a reply or question that would help to continue the conversation. Two have been done as examples.

Conversation starter	Question tag	Reply (giving additional information)
1) It's been quite cold today, hasn't it?		Yes, it certainly has, and I was outside gardening all day.
2) John is a great cook,	_____ ?	Yes, he is. Have you known him for a long time?
3) It's a great party,	_____ ?	_____
4) That music was great,	_____ ?	_____

Strategies to keep a conversation going	Examples
Ask questions – keep them general rather than personal.	'What kind of work do you do?' 'Have you lived in this area very long?'
Give appropriate feedback to show you are listening and interested.	'Really?' 'That's interesting'. 'Yes, I know what you mean.'
Use appropriate 'non-verbal' feedback (also called 'body language') to show you are interested.	Smile and nod your head appropriately to show you are listening. Note: Different cultures have different ideas about what is appropriate 'body language'. For example, speakers in some cultures stand quite close to their partner when speaking, whereas in other cultures, speakers stand a further distance apart.
When asked a question, give an extended answer, rather than a short 'yes' or 'no' reply.	Question: 'Do you like it here?' Reply: 'Yes. The thing I like the most is the weather. I really enjoy…

When you have said all you want to say about a topic, either change to another topic,
       or
  excuse yourself:
	On another topic,… have you been following the tennis?
	
	Excuse me, I need to speak to …over there before they leave.

D) Phrasal verbs – a note on correct word order

In Unit 5 your learned that in English it is common to use words such as 'up', 'in', 'on', after verbs to express a variety of meanings. For example, 'come in' is another way of saying 'enter'. These 'two word verbs' are called **phrasal verbs**. As there are many phrasal verbs in English, students should try to learn the meaning of each expression as it is encountered in context.

It is important to note that when the object of the verb is replaced with a pronoun (it, her, him etc), the position of the pronoun is generally immediately after the verb.

For example, in the sentence: 'We've been *doing up*∗ the house. The word 'house' is the object. So if we use 'it' in place of the word 'house', the word order of the sentence will change.

eg. We've been *doing up*∗ **the house**' becomes 'We've been *doing it up*.' Notice that the pronoun 'it' directly follows the verb.

The sentence: 'We've been *doing up it*.', with the pronoun at the end of the phrase is **incorrect**.

∗doing up = repairing/improving

Practice

Rewrite the sentences using a pronoun in place of the underlined object.
The first one has been done as an example.

1) We **brought up** the boys in Hawaii. _____ We *brought **them** up* in Hawaii.

2) Have you **tried on** your new coat yet? _____

3) I **pick up** my son from school everyday. _____

4) I can't **work out** this problem. _____

5) He **called off** our appointment. _____

6) When did you **do up** the house? _____

Answers: page 120.

Note:
The pattern above applies to phrasal verbs functioning as transitive verbs where the object is replaced with a pronoun. Many modern dictionaries now list phrasal verbs and show their grammatical structure.

(Units 7 – 9)

This section reviews some of the expressions that were introduced in Units 7, 8, and 9 and gives you a chance to see what you have remembered.

Look at the pictures on the opposite page and decide what the people are saying by choosing from the expressions below.

Match each picture with an appropriate expression by writing the correct letter in the box next to each expression.

For extra practice, you could write the appropriate expression in the space provided in the picture.

1) I'm in a fix! What am I going to do now? ☐

2) Oh no! I think I've let the cat out of the bag. ☐

3) I'm going to take it easy this afternoon. ☐

4) No thanks - anything containing egg doesn't agree with me. ☐

5) I love it here. I know we have to rough it but I'm in my element. ☐

6) You can say that again! I'm having a great time! ☐

7) Here's Paul now. He's been on the go all day, sorting out a problem at work. ☐

8) I'm snowed under here at the office so I'll be home late. ☐

9) Sorry I didn't catch that. It's a bit noisy in here. ☐

(Answers: page 121)

PART - 1

1) a) a new job   2) b) a computer course

3) a) he is too old to learn new things, & c) he will enquire about a course this week

PART - 5 CROSSWORD

						8			10			12				
						g			b			s				
					¹g	e	t	*	t	h	e	*	h	a	n	g	*	o	f

Crossword grid:

- 8 down: g e t t i n g *
- 10 down: b y o n d * m e
- 12 down: s m e *
- 1 across: get * the * hang * of
- 4 down: s i c k * a t t *
- 3 across: catch * on
- 6 down: s w i g
- 2 down: i n * a r u *
- 5 across: buzz
- 7 across: head * nor * tail
- 9 across: tons (with b o a down from 5)
- 11 across: the * first * thing

PART - 6   FOCUS ON SPOKEN LANGUAGE

A) 'Hello' has two syllables.

B) There are 24 contractions in Conversation 1

Full form	Contraction	How many syllables in the contracted form?
I would..................	I'd	1
you are.....................	you're	1
I am........................	I'm	1
could not.....................	couldn't	2
what have.................	what've	2
do not.....................	don't	1
it is............................	it's	1
you will	you'll	1
you have......................	you've	1
I had....................	I'd	1
we are.....................	we're	1
I will........................	I'll	1

PART - 1

They are talking about the first photo, which is a photo of Jane's two sons.

in-laws   - people related by marriage   (cultural) background - person's origin
characteristic   - usual feature in appearance/habit   tolerant - respectful of other's beliefs/ideas
relationship   - association/friendship between people

1) b) a few months ago   2) c) a heart problem   3) b) cultural differences

PART - 5 CROSSWORD

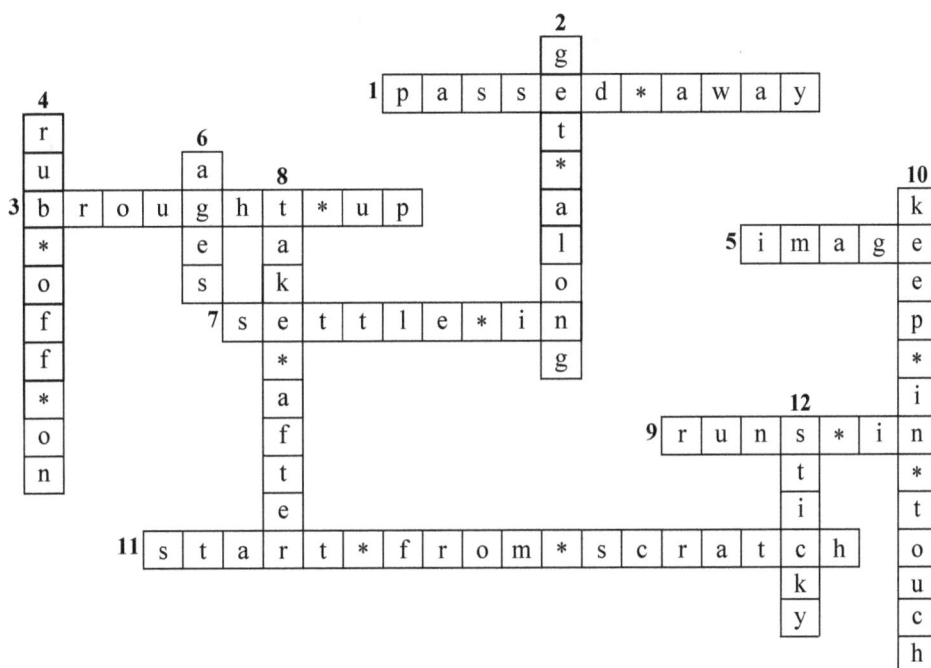

```
                                        2
                                        g
                             1 p a s s e d * a w a y
     4                                  t
     r          6                       *
     u          a          8           a
  3 b r o u g h t * u p                 l                    10
     *          e         a             o         5 i m a g e k
     o          s         k             n                      e
     f         7 s e t t l e * i                               e
     f          *         *             g                      p
     *          a                             12              *
     o          f                   9 r u n s * i n            i
     n          t                             t               *
                e                             i               t
 11 s t a r t * f r o m * s c r a t c h       c               o
                                              k               u
                                              y               c
                                                              h
```

PART - 6   FOCUS ON SPOKEN LANGUAGE

A) 'Question tags' in conversational speech

1) He's the image of his father isn't he?   Yes, he is.

2) He wasn't very old, was he?   No, he wasn't - only 38.

_____

a) In-laws can be a problem, can't they?   Yes, they can.

b) It was cold today, wasn't it?   Yes, it was.

c) This classroom isn't very big. is it?   No, it isn't.

B) Hearing and pronouncing syllables correctly

Merv: Are **these** your **sons**, Jean? I haven't seen them for **ages**.

Jean: Yes, that **photo** was **taken** a few months **ago**.

Merv: John hasn't changed a bit. He's the **image** of his **father**, isn't he?

Jean: Yes, he is. He **takes** after his father, that's for **sure**.

Merv: What's he **doing** these days?

Jane: He's **followed** in his father's footsteps too and works in the **family** **importing**

business. He's living **overseas** at the **moment**.

*For information on the pronunciation of words with 'ed' endings see Unit 8, Part 6D.

PART - 1

1) b) not very happy

2) c) likes the people who live on one side of her house but doesn't like the people on the other side.

3) a) he hasn't met the new people yet.

4) c) is probably watching her and Bob.

PART - 5   CROSSWORD

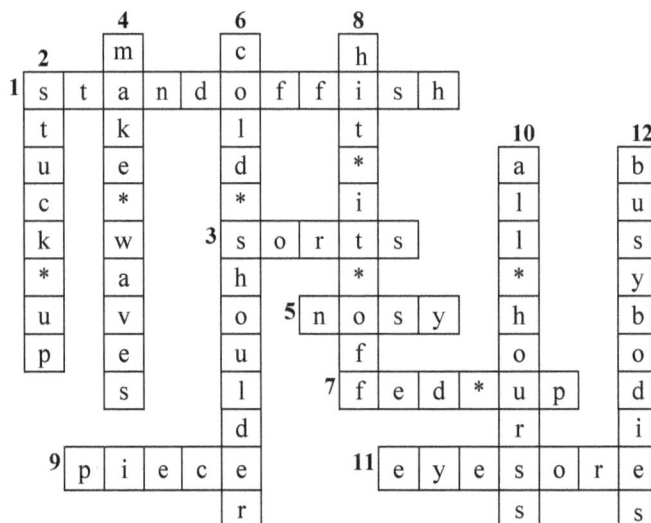

```
            4         6         8
       2    m         c         h
   1  s  t  a  n  d  o  f  f  i  s  h
                               10        12
       t    k         l         t    a     b
       u    e         d         i    l     u
       c    *         *         i    l     s
       k    w      3  s  o  r  t  s   *     y
       *    a         h         *    h     b
       u    v         o      5  n  o  s  y  o
       p    e         u         f    o     o
            s         l      7  f  e  d  *  u  p   d
                      d               r     i
       9  p  i  e  c  e      11  e  y  e  s  o  r  e
                      r               s     s
```

PART - 6   FOCUS ON SPOKEN LANGUAGE

A) Using Pronouns

1) *They* refers to 'the people next door who were making a racket'.

2) *They* refers to 'the people next door who were making a racket'.

3) *They* refers to 'Chris and Tom'.

4) *They* refers to 'Chris and Tom'.

5) *They* refers to 'the new people next door to Bob'.

6) *They* refers to 'the new people next door to Bob'.

B) Pronouns - pronunciation and spelling
Practice

1) *We're* very upset because we lost our camera when we *were* overseas last month.

2) *He's* very happy that he's passed *his* driving test!

3) *You're* much taller than *your* sister but she's older than you, isn't she?

4) The cat has eaten *its* dinner and now *it's* sitting under the tree.

5) *They're* coming by train because *their* car is being repaired.

C) Changing the topic during a conversation

By the way, what are the new people next door to you like Bob?

D) Giving an opinion

So I think they're stuck up, if you ask me.

LANGUAGE REVIEW ONE

1) F	4) H	7) C
2) D	5) E	8) B
3) A	6) I	9) G

PART - 1

1) b) a pair of shoes   3) a) both enjoy shopping
2) a) before they start shopping   4) c) two thirty

PART - 5   CROSSWORD

```
      2        4                          6        8
  1 | s  p  u  r  *  o  f  *  t  h  e  *  m  o  m  e  n  t |
    |    p     i                          e        t  h  |   (e)(h)
    |    e   3 p  i  c  k  *  u  p         n        e     |
    |    n     *            10             d        *     |
    |    d   5 c  o  n  n  e  d  *  i  n  t  o  *    k     |
    |    i     f            e              m        n     |
    |    n     f            l   7 p  u  s  h  y      a     |
    |    g              i     i            *        c     |
    |    *                                 w        k     |
  9 |    s  h  o  p  *  a  r  o  u  n  d    a        *     |
    |    p                                 y        o     |
 11 | a  r  m  *  a  n  d  *  a  *  l  e  g  s        f     |
    |    e                                               |
    |    e                                               |
```

Across:
1 spur * of * the * moment
3 pick * up
5 conned * into
7 pushy
9 shop * around
11 arm * and * a * leg

PART - 6   FOCUS ON SPOKEN LANGUAGE

A) Question tags - Revision

	Statement	Question tag	Short reply
1)	Some shoes are a rip-off,	aren't they?	(No reply)
2)	You won't get carried away with your shopping and lose track of time, will you?		Don't worry, I won't….

C) Developing awareness of 'weak forms' in spoken English

Mari: I'm <u>a</u> bit broke <u>at</u> <u>the</u> moment Ingrid, so I don't want <u>to</u> spend too much today but I'd like <u>to</u> shop around <u>for</u> <u>a</u> pair <u>of</u> shoes that don't cost <u>an</u> arm <u>and</u> <u>a</u> leg.

PART - 1

virus - a sickness caused by a germ/micro-organism

symptoms - signs or changes to the health of a person

prescription - a doctor's written instruction for the use of medicine

examination - a careful inspection

1) c) her son is sick & d) she feels unwell   2) b) a headache   3) b) have a few days off work

PART - 5   CROSSWORD

```
        2         4                         6
        u       1 c  l  e  a  r  *  u  p              8
        n         o                      i        10    f
        d         m                      c        k     i
        e         e                      k        e     t
      3 r  u  n  * d  o  w  n             *        e     *
        *         d                      u        e     a
        t         o                      p        p     s
      5 t  h  r  o  w  *  u  p                     *     a
        e         n                               a     *
      7 c  o  m  e  *  u  p  *  w  i  t  h         n     f
        w         w                               *     i
        e         i                 9 o  n  * t  h  e  * m  e  n  d
        a         t                               e     d
        t         h                               *     d
        h                                         o     l
     11 o  v  e  r  d  o  i  n  g  *  i  t         n     e
        r
```

PART - 6   FOCUS ON SPOKEN LANGUAGE

A) Some intonation patterns of English

Doctor:	And when did these symptoms come on?
Mrs. Smith:	About five days ago.... but I've been having bad headaches for a while now.
Doctor:	Mm. Have you been overdoing it lately? Are you worrying about something?
Mrs Smith:	I suppose I am. I've been pretty uptight lately about work at the office.

B) Incomplete sentences in spoken language

Doctor:	Mm. Have you been overdoing it lately? Are you worrying about something?
Mrs Smith:	I suppose I am *worrying about something*.

C) Phrasal verbs

1) He's <u>picked up</u> a lot today.   *improved*

2) And when did these symptoms <u>come on</u>?   *begin*

3) If the problem doesn't <u>clear up</u> in a few days we'll run some tests.   *become better*

D) Stages in a medical consultation

Doctor:	What seems to be the problem, Mrs Smith?	**1**
Mrs. Smith:	Well actually, it's my son. He's had a fever since Wednesday and he's been *throwing up*. He's *picked up* a bit today but he's still *under the weather*.	**2**
Doctor:	Mm. He could have the *bug* that's going around.	**4**
	Pop him on the table and I'll give him *a check up*. Has he complained about a sore *tummy?*	**3**
Mrs. Smith:	He did yesterday - not so much today.	**2**
Doctor:	Mm. Just *keep an eye on* him. I'll give you a prescription for some medicine but I think he's *on the mend*.	**4/5**
	Is there anything else?	**1**
Mrs. Smith:	Yes. I'd like you to *take a look at* me while I'm here. I think I'm coming *down with something*. Usually I'm *as fit as a fiddle* but the last couple of days I've been feeling really *off*.	**2**
Doctor:	Mm. It could be the same bug....	**4**
	Any other symptoms?	**1**
Mrs. Smith: Doctor: Mrs. Smith: Doctor: Mrs. Smith:	Yes. I feel really *run down* and I've had *a splitting headache*. And when did these symptoms *come on?* About five days ago.... but I've been having bad headaches for a while now. Mm. Have you been *overdoing it* lately? Are you worrying about something? I suppose I am. I've been *pretty uptight* lately about work at the office.	**2**
Doctor	Well, first of all, I think you need a few days off work to *take it easy*. If the problem doesn't *clear up* in a few days we'll run some tests and see what we *come up with*.	**5**
Mrs. Smith: Doctor:	OK. Thank you Doctor. Give me a call......	**6**

ANSWERS TO UNIT SIX - WORRYING ABOUT MONEY

PART - 1

1) b) at home
2) a) household bills
3) b) have similar opinions

PART - 5   CROSSWORD

```
                                       2
 1 f  a  l  l  *  b  a  c  k  *  o  n
                                    e
             6           8          s                            12
          4     b           p       t                             g
             c  r           u       *           10                o
 3 t  h  r  o  u  g  h  *  t  h  e  *  r  o  o  f                  *
             i  k           *       g                             e
             p  e           a       g                             a
             *              w     5 w  h  o  *  k  n  o  w  s      s
             i              a           *                         y
             n  7 g  e  t  *  b  y   9 u  p  *  t  o  *  o  u  r  * e  a  r  s
                                        u                          *
          11 m  a  k  e  *  e  n  d  s  *  m  e  e  t               o
                                                                   n
```

PART - 6 FOCUS ON SPOKEN LANGUAGE

A) Giving feedback The following expressions are all forms of 'feedback' that indicate agreement:
1. Mm. I know what you mean.
2. Yes OK.
3. Well, better still…   (This indicates agreement but then introduces a 'better' idea.)
4. Mm, that sounds fair enough to me.
   Note: Maybe, who knows. (This indicates a 'neutral' position – neither agreeing nor disagreeing.)

B) Giving reasons – justifying actions or opinions

1) We could ask them to chip in for the phone bill, _seeing they're the ones who are on the phone for hours_…

2) He thinks they should chip in for part of the phone bill _seeing they're both working part-time now._

C) Making suggestions

1) Maybe we '_d better_ sit down and work out a budget.

2) We'll **have to** talk to the kids about going easy on their phone calls in future.

3) Well, better still, we **could** ask them to chip in for the phone bill ….

- '_will have to_' + verb indicates the greatest degree of certainty.

LANGUAGE REVIEW TWO

1) D	4) I	7) A
2) H	5) C	8) F
3) B	6) E	9) G

ANSWERS TO UNIT SEVEN - TALKING ABOUT PLACES AND PREFERENCES

PART – 1   A) luxury, resort   B) remote, camping

1) b) Friday
2) b) travel plans & preferred leisure activities
3) b) a year
4) a) have different ideas about leisure activities

PART - 5   CROSSWORD

```
                                                      4                        6
                              2                       r                        r
        8    1 l e t * t h e * c a t * o u t * o f * t h e * b a g
        u                     a                       u            10          t
        p                     k              3 o n * t h e * g o   l           *
        *                     e                       h            i           r
        t                     *                       *            v           a
        h    5 s p i l l * t h e * b e a n s          i            e           c
        e                     t                       t            *           e
        *                     *                                    i
      7 w a i t e d * o n * h a n d * a n d * f o o t              t
        a                     a                                    *
        l                     s                                    u
        l                     y              9 u n d e r * w r a p s
```

PART - 6 FOCUS ON SPOKEN LANGUAGE

B) Talking about preferences

> John: I want to see as much of the world as possible but I want to get off the beaten track and away from the rat race of city life.
>
> Susan: Well, it sounds like you'll be on the go.
>
> John: I sure will and I'll have to rough it but I love camping so I'll be in my element!
>
> Susan: Really?..... Well, that's not my idea of a fun time. I**'d** prefer to live it up at a resort where I**'d** be waited on hand and foot. Somewhere I could let my hair down, party at night and then take it easy beside the pool during the day.
>
> John: Oh no. It**'d** drive me up the wall to lie around a pool all day. That's not my cup of tea at all.
>
> Susan: Oh well, to each his own. I'll see you on Saturday anyway. Oh, and please don't tell anyone I let the cat out of the bag.
>
> John: Don't worry, I won't. I'll definitely keep it under wraps.

Ways of expressing preference:

1) I**'d prefer to live it up** at a resort.

In Sentence 1), 'prefer' is followed by 'to' + verb. This structure **to + verb** is referred to as the *infinitive* in grammar books.

C) Ellipsis – leaving words out in short replies

I sure will <u>be on the go</u>.
Don't worry. I won't <u>tell anyone you let the cat out of the bag</u>.

ANSWERS TO UNIT 8 - MAKING AN ARRANGEMENT BY TELEPHONE

PART - 1

1) b) a plumber   2) b) 5 o'clock   3) a) Mr Ford

PART - 5   CROSSWORD

		2								4			8			
		s						6		g						
		n	¹h	o	l	d	*	t	h	e	*	l	i	n	e	
10		w						f		t					m	
³c	a	l	l	e	d	*	o	f	f		f	*		a		
a		d						y		i			k			
t	⁵a	*	g	o	o	d	*	r	u	n		n			e	
c		u								*			*			
h		n		12					⁷s	o	r	t	*	o	u	t	i
		d		a						o						
⁹t	a	k	e	*	a	*	l	o	o	k		u				
		r		f								c				
				i	¹¹a	*	r	o	u	g	h	*	i	d	e	a
				x												

© Boyer Educational Resources

PART 6 - FOCUS ON SPOKEN LANGUAGE

A) Making an arrangement by telephone

Receptionist:	Good afternoon, Davison's Plumbing. Hold the line please... Sorry to keep you waiting. Can I help you?	**1**
Customer:	Yes. Is that Davison's Plumbing?	
Receptionist:	Yes, it is.	
Customer:	I'd like a plumber to take a look at my toilet please. It seems to be blocked.	**2**
Receptionist:	Certainly. We're a bit snowed under this afternoon so the plumber may not be able to make it there until tomorrow. Is that OK?	
Customer:	Not really. We're in a fix because we've only got one toilet. Is it possible for him to come sooner?	
Receptionist:	Mm. It's a bit iffy, I'm sorry. He's completely tied up with appointments all day…but look, if you'd like to hang on a minute, I'll try to get in touch with him and see how he's fixed for time.	**3**
Customer:	OK. Thank you.	
Receptionist:	Hello ....Well you're in luck. He's had a good run with his work today and his last appointment was called off, so he can fit you in at about 5 o'clock	
Customer:	Oh great! Could you give me a rough idea of the cost?	
Receptionist:	No sorry, not until he sorts out the cause of the problem but don't worry he'll fill you in on the cost before he goes ahead with the work.	
Customer:	OK. Thanks very much for your help.	
Receptionist:	You're welcome. Could I have your name and address please?	
Customer:	Yes, it's Mr. Ford.	
Receptionist:	Sorry, I didn't catch that. Did you say Sword.?	
Customer:	No. Ford. F for father,-O-R-D. My address is number 12 Mar Street, Newtown.	**4**
Receptionist:	Could you spell the name of your suburb please.	
Customer:	Yes it's N-E-W-T-O-W-N.	
Receptionist:	OK thanks. We'll see you this afternoon, at about 5 o' clock.	
Customer:	OK thanks. Bye	**5**
Receptionist:	Bye.	

B) Checking information given on the telephone

Customer: '*Yes. Is that Davison's Plumbing?*'

C) Using polite language when requesting service

1) Pass me a bag.   *Could you pass me a bag, please?*
2) Give the manager this message.   Could you give the manager this message, please?
3) Show me the blue shirt there.   Could you show me the blue shirt there, please?
4) Give me a bottle of Coke.   Could I have a bottle of Coke, please?

D) Pronunciation of words ending with 'ed'

The underlined words with 'ed' endings are pronounced as **one** syllable. The 'ed' ending is pronounced as part of the preceding syllable.

Customer:	I'd like a plumber to take a look at my toilet please. It seems to be **blocked**.
Receptionist:	Certainly. We're a bit **snowed** under this afternoon so the plumber may not be able to make it there until tomorrow. Is that OK?
Customer:	Not really. We're in a fix because we've only got one toilet. Is it possible for him to come sooner?
Receptionist:	Mm. It's a bit iffy, I'm sorry. He's completely **tied** up with appointments all day... but look, if you'd like to hang on a minute, I'll try to get in touch with him and see how he's **fixed** for time.
Customer:	OK. Thank you…
Receptionist:	… Hello…Well you're in luck. He's had a good run with his work today and his last appointment was **called** off, so he can fit you in at about 5 o'clock.

Practice

'ed' pronounced as an extra syllable (making two-syllable words)	'ed' pronounced as part of the preceding syllable (making one-syllable words)	
needed	worked	phoned
started	looked	washed

ANSWERS TO UNIT NINE - AT A SOCIAL GATHERING

PART - 1

1) b) Kate's husband. 2) b) they are work colleagues (they work for the same company)

3) c) a person they both know, d) their work, e) sport/hobbies, g) local area/home

PART - 5   CROSSWORD

```
        2
        m
        i            4              6
   1    n  o  w  *   a  n  d  *  a   g  a  i  n
        d            *              *
        *            g              c
        y        3   b  e  a  t  s  r
 5  u p * o  n                      e              8
        u            *              d              a
                     t              i              b
   7    g  o  o  d *  p  a  r  t  *  o  f           o
                     g              *              u   10
                     e              t              t   i
   9    t  a  k  e *  y  o  u  *  u  p  *  o  n     t   t
                     h              *              i   o
                     e              y              m
                     r              o
                        11  d  o  *  u  p          e
```

Across: 1) now and again 3) beats 5) up on 7) good part of 9) take you up on 11) do up

Down: 2) mind you 4) a get together 6) a credit to you 8) about time 10) into

PART - 6   FOCUS ON SPOKEN LANGUAGE

A)   Making 'Small Talk' – appropriate topics

Inappropriate questions

- How much do you earn?

- Are you married? ⌉ Some people may think questions about marital/family status are
- Do you have any children? ⌡ personal, so avoid asking if you are unsure.

- Why aren't you married?

- Why don't you have any children?

- How much did your house cost?

- What is your address?   Depending on the situation this question may be too direct or personal. Some people don't like to give their address to someone they don't know well. It would be better to ask something less direct such as: 'Do you live in this area?' 'Did you have to travel very far?' These questions give people the option to give their address *if* they think it is appropriate.

B)   Starting a conversation and keeping it going

Bill: Hello. You must be Len. I'm Bill, Kate's husband.

2 someone they both know	3 work/jobs	5 their hobbies
1 their names (who they are)	4 nearby area/home	6 sport in the news

C)   Revision - Using question tags to begin a conversation

Conversation starter	Question tag	Reply (giving additional information or continuing the conversation)
		Various answers are possible. Some possible replies are:
1) It's been quite cold today,	hasn't it?	Yes, it certainly has, and I was outside gardening all day.
2) John is a great cook,	isn't he?	Yes, he is. Have you known him for a long time?
3) It's a great party,	isn't it?	Yes, I'm having a great time. Do you know many people here?
4) That music was great,	wasn't it?	Yes, I love the saxophone. Do you play a musical instrument?

D) Phrasal verbs   **Answers**

1) We ***brought up*** <u>the boys</u> in Hawaii.   We ***brought <u>them</u> up*** in Hawaii.

2) Have you ***tried on*** <u>your new coat</u> yet?   Have you ***tried <u>it</u> on*** yet?

3) I ***pick up*** <u>my son</u> from school everyday.   I ***pick <u>him</u> up*** from school everyday.

4) I can't ***work out*** <u>this problem</u>.   I can't ***work <u>it</u> out*** .

5) He ***called off*** <u>our appointment</u>.   He ***called <u>it</u> off.***

6) When did you ***do up*** <u>the house</u>?   When did you ***do <u>it</u> up***?

1)	A	6)	F
2)	I	7)	G
3)	C	8)	H
4)	B	9)	E
5)	D		

EVERYDAY EXPRESSIONS	DEFINITIONS
give (someone) a buzz	call (someone) on the telephone
get into the swing of things	become familiar with the usual way to do things
hassles	problems/difficulties
be beyond (someone)	be too difficult for (someone)
not make head or tail of (something)	not understand anything about
stuck at it	kept trying
Good for you!	Congratulations!
What have you been up to?	What have you been doing?
in a rut	in a boring pattern of doing things
don't know the first thing about (something)	**don't** know anything about (something)
catch on	learns/understands
Come off it!	Oh, I don't agree with you!
tons	a lot of
in the same boat	in the same situation
Go on!	You should do it!
get the hang of it	understand what to do
talked (me) into it	convinced (me) to do something
getting along	progressing/managing
See you	Goodbye

*Where a word appears between brackets (   ) in reference lists, it means that other pronouns or nouns may also be used in the expression.

EVERYDAY EXPRESSIONS	DEFINITIONS
for ages..	for a long time
the image of (someone)..................................	the same in appearance
take after..	is similar to (an older family member)
these days..	the present time
has followed in (someone's) footsteps............	has done the same as (someone)
start from scratch..	start from the beginning without help
settled in..	become established
runs in (the family).......................................	is a common characteristic in (the family)
passed away..	died
keep in touch……………………………..	communicate regularly
don't get along......................……………	don't like (another person)
sticky (situation)...	difficult (situation)
You're kidding?..…..	Really? That is difficult to believe/understand
a tough one...	a difficult problem
brought up (children).....................................	trained and educated (in the family)
get on with ....….…….	be friendly with/ be compatible with
rub off on..	have an influence on

EVERYDAY EXPRESSIONS	DEFINITIONS
out of sorts..............................	unhappy/unwell
didn't sleep a wink	didn't sleep at all
a racket....................................	a lot of noise
all hours………………………………..	very late at night
couldn't care less………………………	don't care
fed up......................................	very unhappy
give (them) a piece of your mind……..	tell (them) you are displeased/upset
make waves..	cause trouble
wouldn't take any notice………………	wouldn't listen/act on
way-out....................................	strange/unusual
eyesore…………………………………..	an ugly thing/place to look at
*hit it off...............………........……….	like each other
terrific...............………........................	excellent
standoffish..	unfriendly
give (me) the cold shoulder..................	deliberately ignore (me)
stuck up.............................……………	think they are superior
nosy…………...............………………….	inquisitive (describing a person who is always watching what other people are doing)
a busybody.............................…………	interfering person who wants to know about others
going on..............................……………	happening

Note:
*'hit it off', meaning 'like each other', can also be expressed in the negative:
'don't hit it off', meaning '**don't** like each other'

EVERYDAY EXPRESSIONS	DEFINITIONS
a bit broke	to not have much money
shop around	visit a few shops to look for the best price
cost an arm and a leg	cost a lot of money/too much money
a rip-off	overpriced
(to) check out	look at/investigate
the deli	delicatessen
pricey	expensive
pushy	very persistent
pick up	get/collect
bits and pieces	small items
What are you after?	What are you looking for?
a spending spree	an enjoyable time spending money
the knack of	the ability/skill
conned into	persuaded/tricked into doing something unwise
more often than not	often/usually
on the spur of the moment	on impulse
mend (my) ways	reform/improve my habits
get carried away	become too interested/involved
*lose track of (time)	forget about (time) because of a distraction

*Note: The expression 'lose track of ...' can also be used to talk about a *person* (rather than 'time'
In this case it means to lose contact/communication with a person.
eg. 'I've *lost track* of my school friends. I haven't seen then for six years'.

EVERYDAY EXPRESSIONS	DEFINITIONS
throwing up	vomiting
picked up	improved
under the weather	unwell/sick
a/the bug	virus
pop	put (something somewhere)
a check-up	a medical examination
tummy	stomach
keep an eye on	keep a careful watch
on the mend	improving in health
take a look at	examine
coming down with (something)	getting a sickness
fit as a fiddle	very healthy
off	unwell
run-down	unwell/tired
a splitting headache	a very bad headache
come on	begin/start
overdoing it	working too hard
pretty uptight	quite anxious
take it easy	relax/rest
clear up	become better
come up with	find/discover

EVERYDAY EXPRESSIONS	DEFINITIONS
gone through the roof..................	reached a very high price
to get ahead....................…........	progress financially
figure out.......…...........……........	understand
forking out ....….........……	unwillingly/reluctantly paying
work out ....….........	plan the details
It's got me beat................................	I don't understand
well off ....…….......	wealthy
splurged... ....…............	spent a lot of money
can't make ends meet..........…...……	are not able to pay living expenses
up to (their) ears in (something).......	deeply involved in (something)
for all we know.....……................	we don't really know
who knows.........................…....…	I don't know the answer to that
get by......................…........………	to manage (a difficult situation) without difficulty
to put away (money)...............….....	save (money)
(build) a nest egg................……......	get/have money saved for the future
something to fall back on.................	a reserve for future use
flat broke.......................................	having no money
go easy on (something)...........….…..	use less/spend less of (something)
chip in..	contribute
chatting........…….................………	talking informally

EVERYDAY EXPRESSIONS	DEFINITIONS
a send-off.................................………	a farewell party
let the cat out of the bag....................	revealed a secret
hush hush..	secret
spill the beans....................................	revealed a secret
off the beaten track...........................	away from populated areas
the rat race......................................……	the constantly busy competition of city life
on the go..	busy
to rough it..	live without basic comforts
in (my) element..................…..........	be in (my) preferred situation
live it up..	live in luxury
be waited on hand and foot..............	have all needs attended to
let (my) hair down...........................	behave very informally
take it easy.......................................	relax/rest
drive (me) up the wall......................	greatly irritate (me)
not my cup of tea.........................……	not something that interests me
to each his own...............................	everyone has their own preference
keep (it) under wraps………………	keep the information a secret

EVERYDAY EXPRESSIONS	DEFINITIONS
Hold the line.......................................	Wait a moment
take a look ....……..	inspect
snowed under....................................	busy (with work)
to make it...	arrive
in a fix..	in a difficult situation
iffy..	uncertain/doubtful
tied up……..	involved with
hang on...	wait
get in touch......................................	contact/speak to (someone)
*see how (he) is fixed for time..	see how much spare time (he) has available
a good run..	good progress
called off..	cancelled
*fit (you) in..................................	make time available for (you)
a rough idea	an approximate idea
sort out...	determines/finds the answer to (something)
*fill (you) in......................................	supply/give (you) information
goes ahead with	starts
catch...	hear/understand

*Where a word appears between brackets ( ) in reference lists, it means that other pronouns may also be used in the expression.

EVERYDAY EXPRESSIONS	DEFINITIONS
about time ………………….…	timely (but it should have happened before now)
a get together................................	a social gathering
showing (me) the ropes.................	explaining to (me) how to do something
a top spot………………………….	a nice place
(has) a lot going for it...................	has a lot of advantages
beats………................................	is better than
You can say that again..................	I agree with you
going on....................………........	almost/approximately
mind you.....................................	but/however
good part of ..………...................	most of/almost
do (something) up	repair/improve (something)
It's a credit to you...........................	It's something you should be very proud of
great...	very good/excellent
have my wits about me..................	be alert/clear in my head
now and again..............................	sometimes/occasionally
I'll take you up on that………….…	I'll accept that offer.
be up on (something) ……………	be knowledgeable about (something)
once in a while……………………	occasionally
be into (something)………………	interested in/involved in (something)

Reference page
Some notable pronunciation differences between varieties of English

Words containing the letter 'a'

Many English words, containing the letter 'a', may be pronounced as a short sound /æ/ or a long sound /ɑ:/ depending on which variety of English is being spoken. See the table below which shows examples of pronunciation differences across varieties of English.

Spelling	Examples of pronunciation differences for the following words.		
ask passed last laugh can't half plant	/æsk/ /pæst/ /læst/ /læf/ /kænt/ /hæf/ /plænt/	may be pronounced as the vowel sound /æ/ as in *bl**a**ck h**a**t*.	/ɑ:sk/ /pɑ:st/ /lɑ:st/ /lɑ:f/ /kɑ:nt/ /hɑ:f/ /plɑ:nt/ may be pronounced as the lengthened vowel sound /ɑ:/ as in *large h**ear**t.*

Words containing the letter 'o'

There are differences between North American English and British English in the pronunciation of some words containing the letter 'o'. For example, in British English, the words *st**o**p*, *d**o**t*, *l**o**ck* are pronounced with the vowel sound /ɒ/. These words, in North American English, are pronounced with the vowel sound /ɑ/, a slightly longer sound. For example, in North American English the words *lock* and *lark* are pronounced with the same vowel sound /ɑ/, whereas in British English *lock* is pronounced /lɒk/ and *lark* is pronounced /lɑ:k/.

Words containing the letter 'r'

In all varieties of English, the letter 'r' in written words, is pronounced clearly in speech when followed by a vowel sound. For example, 'r' is generally pronounced clearly where it is followed by a vowel sound in the same word, eg. **r**ight, **r**oll, pa**r**ag**r**aph; or when 'r' is followed by a vowel sound in the following word, eg. wea**r** it; doo**r** open; fo**r** example.

However, where the letter 'r' is followed by a consonant sound or when it occurs at the end of an utterance, speakers of some varieties of English (Australian/South African/Southern British and other varieties) omit the sound /r/. Speakers of North American English (and other varieties), on the other hand, always pronounce 'r', regardless of its position in a word or utterance.

Spelling	Examples of pronunciation differences for words containing the letter 'r'		
car sport sister four	/kɑ:r/ /spɔ:rt/ /sɪstər/ /fɔ:r/	Generally, speakers of North American, Canadian, Scottish, Irish (and others) pronounce the letter 'r' regardless of its position in a word.	/kɑ:/ /spɔ:t/ /sɪstə/ /fɔ:/ Generally, speakers of Australian, Southern British, South African, and New Zealand English do **not** pronounce 'r' when it is followed by a consonant sound.

Phonemic Chart of English Sounds

Below each sound symbol are examples of words containing the sound.

Vowel sounds

æ (short sound)	e (short sound)	ɒ (not used in USA)	ə (unstressed sound)
black h<u>a</u>t	r<u>e</u>d h<u>ea</u>d	.... d<u>o</u>ts & sp<u>o</u>ts....	oth<u>er</u> broth<u>er</u>
ɑː (long sound)	ʊ (short sound)	ʌ (short sound)	I (short sound)
*f<u>ar</u> st<u>ar</u>	g<u>oo</u>d f<u>oo</u>t	f<u>u</u>n r<u>u</u>n	p<u>i</u>nk b<u>ui</u>lding
3ː (long sound)	uː (long sound)	ɔː (long sound)	iː (long sound)
*p<u>ur</u>ple sk<u>ir</u>t	bl<u>ue</u> m<u>oo</u>n	*f<u>our</u> m<u>ore</u>	r<u>ea</u>l gr<u>ee</u>n

As the pronunciation of some English vowel sounds varies across and within countries, the example words are intended as a *general* guide.

Diphthong (two vowel) sounds

eɪ	ɔɪ	əʊ (also oʊ)	ɪə
gr<u>ey</u> d<u>ay</u>	n<u>oi</u>sy b<u>oy</u>	yell<u>ow</u> g<u>o</u>ld	cl<u>ear</u> b<u>ee</u>r
eə (also ɛə)	aɪ	ʊə	aʊ
*f<u>air</u> h<u>air</u>	br<u>i</u>ght l<u>i</u>me	t<u>our</u> (also /tʊr/	br<u>ow</u>n m<u>ou</u>se

Consonant sounds

Note: voiceless sounds are shown in a shaded box.

p	b	t	d
<u>p</u>et <u>p</u>ig	<u>b</u>ig <u>b</u>ag	<u>t</u>ell <u>t</u>wo	<u>d</u>irty <u>d</u>og
tʃ	dʒ	k	g
<u>Ch</u>inese <u>ch</u>ild	<u>j</u>ust <u>j</u>oking	<u>k</u>eep <u>c</u>ool	<u>g</u>ood <u>g</u>irl
f	v	θ	ð
<u>f</u>ill <u>f</u>our	<u>v</u>ery <u>v</u>ivid	<u>th</u>ink <u>th</u>in	o<u>th</u>er bro<u>th</u>er
s	z	ʃ	ʒ
<u>s</u>ad <u>s</u>ong	<u>z</u>ig-<u>z</u>ag	<u>sh</u>ort <u>sh</u>eep	mea<u>s</u>ure A<u>s</u>ia
m	n	ŋ	h
<u>m</u>ilk <u>m</u>an	<u>n</u>o <u>n</u>ever	lo<u>ng</u> so<u>ng</u>	<u>h</u>ot <u>h</u>ill
l	r	w	j
<u>l</u>ittle <u>l</u>ine	<u>r</u>ight <u>r</u>ice	<u>w</u>et <u>w</u>inter	<u>y</u>es <u>y</u>ou

*Note: In some varieties of English, the letter 'r' is clearly pronounced wherever it occurs in words, (eg. st<u>ar</u>, p<u>ur</u>ple, f<u>our</u>), however in some varieties of English, 'r' is only pronounced when it is followed by a vowel sound.

Boyer Educational Resources books and audio CDs

www.boyereducation.com.au   www.englishebooks.com

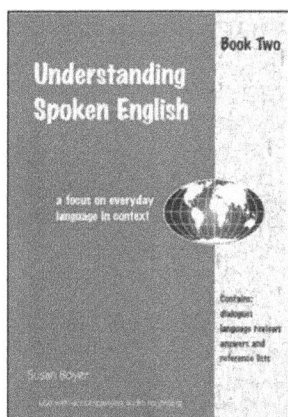

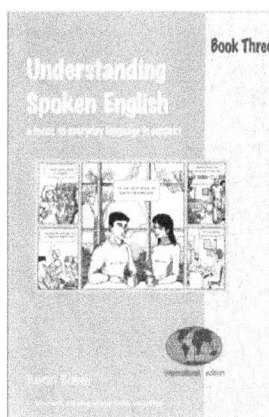

'Understanding Spoken English' – (books with audio CDs)

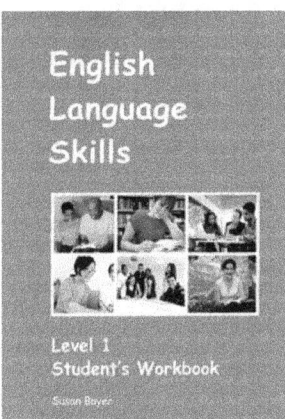

NEW in 2014
Rhyming Stories

includes storybook,
language workbook
and audio CD

**English Language Skills
Level One**

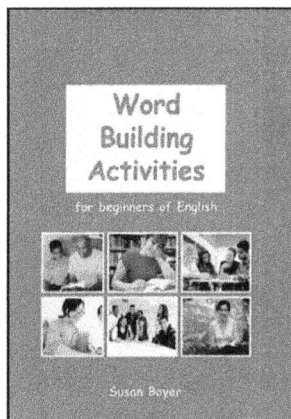

**Word Building Activities
for beginners of English**

**Understanding English
Pronunciation**

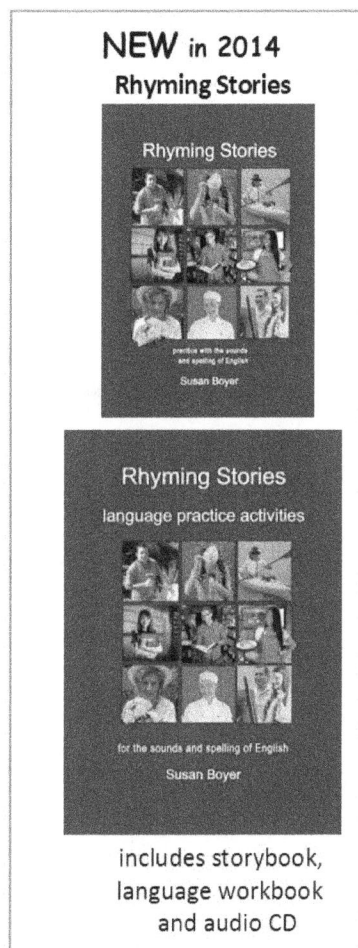

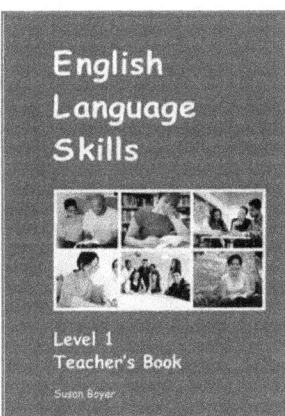

English Language Skills
Teacher's Book

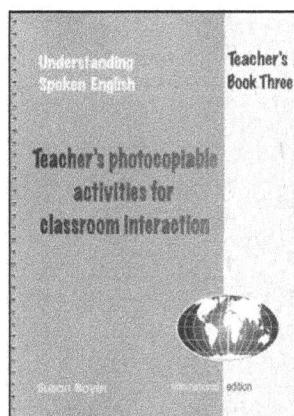

Understanding Spoken English
Teacher's Book

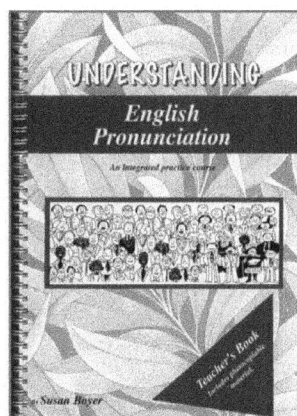

**Understanding English
Pronunciation**
Teacher's Book

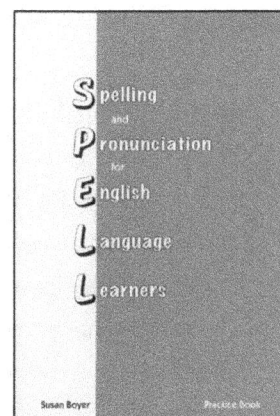

Spelling and Pronunciation
for English Language Learners

Spiral bound Teacher's Books contain photocopiable activity pages, such as surveys,
role cards & matching activities. All our teacher's books are A4 size.
Student books contain language exercises and answers.

www.boyereducation.com for details of all publications by Boyer Educational Resources

www.englishebooks.com for details of e-book versions of these resources

📚 **Boyer Educational Resources**

Office phone/fax: +61 (0)2 4739 1538   e-mail: boyer@eftel.net.au
websites: www.boyereducation.com.au   www.englishebooks.com

Title	ISBN
Rhyming Stories - practice with the sounds and spelling of English (A5)	978 1 877074 06 6
Rhyming Stories -audio CD	978 1 877074 37 0
Rhyming Stories - language workbook (A4)	978 1 877074 38 7
Understanding Spoken English - Book One	978 1 877074 08 0
Understanding Spoken English - Audio CD One (1)	978 1 877074 10 3
Understanding Spoken English - Teacher's Book One	978 1 877074 11 0
Understanding Spoken English – Book One & Audio CD	**978 1 877074 18 9**
Understanding Spoken English - Book Two	978 1 877074 12 7
Understanding Spoken English - Audio CD Two (1)	978 1 877074 14 1
Understanding Spoken English - Teacher's Book Two	978 1 877074 15 8
Understanding Spoken English – Book Two & Audio CD	**978 1 877074 19 6**
Understanding Spoken English - Book Three	978 1 877074 24 0
Understanding Spoken English - Audio CD Three	978 1 877074 25 7
Understanding Spoken English - Teacher's Book Three	978 1 877074 26 4
Understanding Spoken English – Book Three & Audio CD	**978 1 877074 27 1**
Spelling and Pronunciation for English Language Learners	978 1 877074 04 2
Understanding English Pronunciation - Student book only	978 0 9585395 7 9
Understanding English Pronunciation - Audio CD (Set of 3)	978 1 877074 03 5
Understanding English Pronunciation - Teacher's Book	978 0 9585395 9 3
Word Building Activities for Beginners of English	978 1 877074 28 8
English Language Skills – Level One Student's Workbook	978 1 877074 29 5
English Language Skills – Level One Audio CD	978 1 877074 31 8
English Language Skills – Level One Teacher's Book	978 1 877074 32 5

Resources with an Australian focus:

Title	ISBN
Understanding Everyday Australian - Book One	978 0 9585395 00 0
Understanding Everyday Australian - Audio CD One (1)	978 1 877074 01 1
Understanding Everyday Australian - Teacher's Book One	978 0 9585395 2 4
Understanding Everyday Australian - Book One & Audio CD	**978 1 877074 16 5**
Understanding Everyday Australian - Book Two	978 0 9585395 3 1
Understanding Everyday Australian - Audio CD Two (1)	978 1 877074 02 8
Understanding Everyday Australian - Teacher's Book Two	978 0 9585395 5 5
Understanding Everyday Australian - Book Two & Audio CD Pack	**978 1 877074 17 2**
Understanding Everyday Australian - Book Three	978 1 877074 20 2
Understanding Everyday Australian - Audio CD Three	978 1 877074 21 9
Understanding Everyday Australian - Teacher's Book Three	978 1 877074 22 6
Understanding Everyday Australian - Book Three & Audio CD	**978 1 877074 23 3**
People in Australia's past - their stories, their achievements - A5 Reader	978 1 877074 34 9
People in Australia's past - audio CD	978 1 877074 35 6
People in Australia's past - language workbook A4 (156 pages)	978 1 877074 36 3

Visit our website **www.boyereducation.com.au** for a distributor near you.